SOMETHING TO LOVE

DIANA BENET

SOMETHING TO LOVE

BARBARA PYM'S NOVELS

A LITERARY FRONTIERS EDITION, NO. 27
UNIVERSITY OF MISSOURI PRESS
COLUMBIA, 1986

Library of Congress Cataloging-in-Publication Data

Benet, Diana.
  Something to love.

  1. Pym, Barbara—Criticism and interpretation.
2. Love in Literature.   I. Title.
PR6066.Y58Z59   1986   823'.914   85-20976
ISBN 0-8262-0493-7 (alk. paper)

∞™ This paper meets the minimum requirements of the American
National Standard for Permanence of Paper for Printed Library
Materials, z39.48, 1984.

Acknowledgments
  At an early stage of this project, when a period of six to eight weeks
seemed an intolerable delay, Paul De Angelis of E. P. Dutton let me read
A Very Private Eye in galleys, and I am grateful for his kindness. My work, at
every stage, was made easier and more enjoyable by J. Peter Benet, who
is generous with his help, encouragement, and humor.

FOR CYNTHIA TREVIÑO
AND LINDA TREVIÑO SUAREZ

CONTENTS

NOVELS BY BARBARA PYM

Some Tame Gazelle (1950)
Crampton Hodnet (1985)
Excellent Women (1952)
Jane and Prudence (1953)
Less Than Angels (1955)
A Glass of Blessings (1958)
No Fond Return of Love (1961)
An Unsuitable Attachment (1982)
The Sweet Dove Died (1978)
Quartet in Autumn (1977)
A Few Green Leaves (1980)

I. INTRODUCTION

Barbara Pym's novels center on one great subject. "Some tame gazelle or some gentle dove or even a poodle dog: something to *love*, that was the point." This paraphrase of some lines from a half-remembered poem, which appears in Pym's first novel, is the perfect epigraph for her work as a whole. Although the near-quotation comes from a refinedly repressed spinster given to sighing over the unattainable man of her chaste dreams, she identifies the need whose expression or denial moves, shapes, or disfigures all of Pym's major characters: a glamorous young woman, an inelegant gay man, a retired woman losing her mind, or a country rector—women and men with radically different lives and personalities—all explore, in their individual ways, the guises of love, sought, attained, or frustrated.

Pym looks with a compassionate but penetrating eye at love in its different aspects. Every variety finds a place in her work; the heterosexual and homosexual types—even if we break them down into requited, unrequited, and, somewhere between these, the comfortable ardors of pure fantasy—are only its more obvious kinds. Especially when romantic love fails them or is not an option, for one reason or another, Pym's characters seek or find emotional sustenance in the affections of friendship or family ties; in the Christian love that asks "who is my neighbor?"; in the fondness for "child substitutes," human or not; and in the asexual "unsentimental tenderness . . . expressed in small gestures of solicitude" that one solitary soul might extend to another. *Extend* is the key word: in Pym's universe, the heart and mind require an object as the bridge from their fearful isolation to the world of feeling and caring. The reader might laugh at the unkempt old woman troubled by fleas because she keeps hedgehogs as pets, or at the middle-aged bachelor cooing at the pigeons he feeds daily, but they are comparatively fortunate. The typical quest that animates Pym's characters is primarily to find an emotional context or focal point for themselves; it is sometimes expressed as a desire to

1

touch another life, and maybe even to *matter* by making a difference to another living being. It seems modest enough as a goal, but some characters either do not achieve it or reject it altogether.

In addition to treating the need and expression of love in its romantic or other manifestations, Pym eventually treats its total absence or failure. Characteristically, her forte is comedy: an oldish spinster debates the propriety of knitting a sweater for the married archdeacon whom she's loved for over thirty innocent years; a quiet young woman screws up her courage to buy a lipstick called "Hawaiian Fire"; a food critic served bottled mayonnaise feels a disproportionate rage that sends him, complaining of stress, to the doctor. Exploring her large subject, however, leads Pym to tragedy. Seen in the context of her complete oeuvre, the two tragic novels that are her finest achievements seem to be the natural, almost inevitable, development of the author's treatment of her chosen subject. For all of those often-ridiculous women and men who find something to love, either getting their hearts' desires or coming to terms with substitutes for them, there are others who have nothing to love, or who can love only themselves. Pym's depiction of the desolate sterility enclosing those who fail to bridge the chasm from emotional isolation to relationship is devastating. In retrospect, that tube of "Hawaiian Fire" is still funny, but what it represents is not laughable.

Barbara Pym published ten novels, and an eleventh was published in 1985 after her death. Her work was "discovered" recently in this country, and hailed as a comic masterpiece. This is praise, indeed, and accurate—in part: it fails to take into account the development of the author's vision on two fronts, from a feminine to a universal perspective and from the comic to the tragic mode. Pym's novels tell us a great deal about the lives of women and the problems peculiar to them, but her achievement was to become an astute chronicler of concerns and issues fundamental to both sexes. Her early novels suggest that she considers the inner lives of women her particular province; however, as her confidence in the universality of her vision grows, men become more prominent citizens of that province.

Since we will trace Pym's development from the comic to the tragic, and from a feminine to a universal vision, I shall treat the novels in the order in which she wrote them. *Some Tame Gazelle* was written and revised by November 1935, but a few years passed before its final revision; it was published in 1950. *Crampton Hodnet*, written in 1939–1940, was laid aside in manuscript, and was revised and published in 1985 by Hazel Holt, Pym's literary executor. *Excellent Women, Jane and Prudence, Less Than Angels, A Glass of Blessings*, and *No Fond Return of Love* were written in succession and published in the same order in 1952, 1953, 1955, 1958, and 1961, respectively. Pym completed *An Unsuitable Attachment* in February 1963, and in March it was rejected by Jonathan Cape, the company that had published her previous six novels. From September 1964 to February 1965, she revised her novel, but when it was rejected by yet other publishers, she set it aside. The novel was published, with some deletions made by Hazel Holt, in 1982. Pym started *The Sweet Dove Died* in 1963, and finished the first draft by December 1967. Its revision was completed by May 1969, but by April 1973, it had been rejected by twenty-one publishers.[1] She revised the novel again in 1977, and it was finally published in 1978. *Quartet in Autumn* was begun in October 1973 and accepted for publication in February 1977. She started making preliminary notes for *A Few Green Leaves* by October 1977, and its final draft was completed by October 1979. Barbara Pym died in January 1980, and her last novel was published in the same year.

*   *   *

Reading about the death of Esther Clovis in *A Few Green Leaves*, I understood what television commentators mean when they refer to the death of some public figure marking "the end of an era." It's not exactly a personal sorrow but it's not impersonal, either. How, exactly, did Esther die? How

1. *A Very Private Eye: An Autobiography in Diaries and Letters* (New York: E. P. Dutton, 1984), 273. All page numbers in the text for this book and for Pym's novels refer to the Dutton hardback editions, which are cited in abbreviated form, such as *VPE* for *A Very Private Eye*.

old was she? Had she lived all that time (since *Less Than Angels*) with Gertrude Lydgate? As more questions occurred to me, I felt disgruntled: why hasn't Emma Howick enough sense, I wondered, to think or talk to someone about these things so that I might satisfy at least some of my curiosity about this remarkable woman?

Esther is not the central character in any of Pym's novels. The gruff woman (with hair like a dog), who lives her busy and useful life in the background, achieves her importance precisely by being so often a part of others' stories, by being a link from one novel to another. Pym wrote to Philip Larkin about her use of some characters more than once:

> I'm considering what you said about bringing characters from one's earlier books into later ones and I agree that one does have to be careful. It can be a tiresome affectation. With me it's sometimes laziness—if I need a casual clergyman or anthropologist I just take one from an earlier book. Perhaps really one should take such a very minor character that only the author recognises it, like a kind of superstition or a charm. (*VPE*, 203)

Far from seeming "a tiresome affectation," Pym's habit of using characters more than once (in minor, walk-on roles) helps bind the entirety of her work in a cohesive, comprehensive vision. Each of her novels, however small or large a community it features, creates the sense of a whole society. The recurring characters create the impression of a fully realized world; it is credible and, more important, fitting that Wilmet, Rodney, Piers, and Keith (*GB*) should live in the milieu of Dulcie Mainwaring (*NFR*). These characters already known to us provide a sense of continuity, which adds to the realism of the harmonious created world.

Sometimes, too, since the conclusions of Pym's novels seem indeterminate, these cameo appearances satisfy our curiosity about the fate of certain characters. When familiar personalities appear in subsequent novels, they also help create a sense of perspective. The actions and issues that were primary to them (and to the reader) are restored, by the story presently occupying our consciousness, to their proper place in the ordinary scheme of things. "There are eight million stories in the naked city," a voice used to announce at the beginning of a television show, "and this is

4

one of them": Wilmet's brief appearance in Dulcie's life reminds us that both live and act on the same plane of ordinariness, and this suggests, in turn, that there are many stories like theirs—unspectacular, uncatastrophic, and undeniably significant.

Next to Pym's use of linking characters, the other characteristic that distinguishes her novels is their highly allusive quality. Pym's characters are typically educated people, and many of them remember snatches, at least, from "the greater English poets." The range of their references is impressive, including hymns and popular songs as well as lines or phrases from every kind of literature. Among the many authors mentioned or quoted are Patmore, Shakespeare, Anthony Trollope, Goldsmith, Milton, Charlotte Brontë, Tennyson, Herbert, Charlotte Yonge, Keats, Thomas Gray, Wordsworth, Pope, Rochester, T. S. Eliot, Samuel Johnson, Woolf, Marvell, Arnold, Housman, Browning, Donne, Carew, Henry King, Wyatt, Leigh Hunt, John Cleveland, Drayton, Cowley, Vaughan, Christina Rossetti, and Jane Austen. A full analysis of Pym's allusions would probably extend to a book-length study, but even the unsystematic eye will see that they add irony and comedy, and give insight into the characters: a couple of the heroines, we are told, think they are like or unlike Jane Eyre. Fabian Driver dedicates a book to Prudence with a quotation from Marvell (*JP*) that immediately tells the reader the two self-centered people can never come together, no matter how many romantic gifts they exchange—but neither of them understands the significance of the quotation. The lines Aylwin Forbes (*NFR*) remembers from Thomas Wyatt's "They Flee from Me" underscore his romantic arrogance. Told that Emma Howick (*FGL*) was named for Jane Austen's heroine, we are alert for differences and similarities between the old heroine and the new: Austen never dreamed of her Emma making love in the great outdoors with Frank Churchill, but Pym's Emma follows the pattern of favoring the wrong man before turning to the one who has been right for her all along.

It seems especially appropriate that, in her last novel, Pym gave a formal nod in Austen's direction as her predecessor in the novel of manners. Readers of Pym are reminded of Austen because of her satiric and detailed treatment of a distinc-

5

tive social group, and because of her narrative method. Only two of Pym's novels have first-person narrators. In *Excellent Women*, so much of the action centers on characters other than Mildred that she seems almost secondary, but her point of view is essential to capture the real story of her personal development as she observes and learns from others. Because Wilmet Forsyth, the heroine-narrator of *A Glass of Blessings*, is snobbish, spoiled, and somewhat foolish, she must tell her own story in order to gain our sympathy and understanding in spite of her faults. But the rest of Pym's novels are third-person narratives that employ a shifting point of view. Typically, as in Austen's novels, one character's consciousness is given more prominence than the others', and we come to know this character most fully and sympathetically as the action is filtered primarily through her perspective. Belinda Bede, for instance, is accorded such centrality in *Some Tame Gazelle*; her prominence and the gradual revelation of her nature give the novel, as much as the actual plot does, its development and continuity.

Though Belinda wins our sympathy, Pym does not allow it to be an entirely uncritical acceptance. We gain a measure of detachment and objectivity toward her from the other characters (whose various perspectives also help create the sense of an entire society). Our understanding of her is influenced, for example, by Agatha Hoccleve's opinion that she is well-meaning but "rather a nuisance," and by Henry's feeling that she's "a nice peaceful creature . . . so different from his own admirable wife." Even more than from the other actors in the story, however, we take our bearings from a narrator detached from all the characters by an objective and comic point of view. This, for instance, is the description of Belinda and Harriet watching from a window on the day Agatha leaves for Karlsbad:

> From here there was an excellent view of the vicarage drive and gate. Belinda had brought some brass with her to clean and in the intervals when she stopped her vigorous rubbing to look out of the window, was careful to display the duster in her hand. Harriet stared out quite unashamedly, with nothing in her hand to excuse her presence there. She even had a pair of binoculars, which she was now trying to focus. (*STG*, 70)

As we see in this example, the detached narrator is free to

evaluate her characters implicitly and explicitly and to comment on the action, as she does when she remarks that the sisters' curiosity was "understandable" since a departure includes many things of interest "if one could watch it without any feeling of sorrow or regret." Pym's narrative method consists, usually, of this kind of comic indirection and understatement. It permits her to indicate the laughable little pretenses, incongruities, and hypocrisies of her well-bred and courteous people without seeming intrusive or heavy-handed in the analysis of their minor guilts, sins, and rivalries. *Some Tame Gazelle* typifies the narrative method Pym was to employ and refine in her subsequent novels.

The small community is a central aspect of Pym's novels. In the country, where we expect to find such small circles, and in the city, where we do not, Pym's characters live within, or make efforts to create, or tragically lack, a community. Such a context within which the individual can locate himself in relation to others with similar tastes, backgrounds, and concerns is often provided by the Church. Only in *The Sweet Dove Died* is it not a more or less prominent part of the lives of at least some of the characters. When the Church is not the cohesive element that unites Pym's people into a social group, a literal neighborhood or a field of work or study brings them together, anthropology being the chief of these. Whatever the common factor, most of Pym's characters identify themselves, implicitly or explicitly, according to their standing within or without such a circle. The few who lack such a personal context are usually emotionally impoverished human beings.

Clergymen, anthropologists, and spinsters figure prominently in Pym's novels. Most of her over-thirty characters are eminently decent and prudent middle-class people with no serious financial, legal, medical, or personal problems of the type that call for overwhelming sorrows, exertions, or heroics. Mildred Lathbury, reflecting on a friend's energetic battle over a trivial matter, might be speaking for the majority of Pym's characters:

> After all, life was like that for most of us—the small unpleasantnesses rather than the great tragedies; the little useless longings rather than the great renunciations and dramatic love affairs of history or fiction. (*EW*, 101)

7

If we add, following her lead, "the small joys and mundane pleasures rather than the great raptures; the vital little successes rather than the great triumphs," the description is practically complete. Such undramatic people and material will sound bland only to those unacquainted with the novels: these characters with more than a touch of starch or mustard, bringing an energetic zest to bear on trivial and medium-sized problems, are never dull. In her comic novels, Pym treats them with an irreverent levity that reveals their absurdities without diminishing their humanity.

As my analysis of the separate novels will indicate, Pym's women cover a wide range of types. But it is possible to make some generalizations about her heroines, of which the most important is that they are not conventional romantic heroines. Only three, Prudence Bates (*JP*), Wilmet Forsyth (*GB*), and Leonora Eyre (*SDD*) might be considered glamorous, and the first has no interest in marriage, the second is already married, and the third is almost fifty and considers marriage only in a wild fantasy. Five of them desire matrimony or a significant relationship with a man, but only one of these actually marries in the novel in which she is prominent. Most of them are sociable, sensitive, and literate women with a good sense of humor, who have either no interest or no talent in the art of "making the most" of themselves—multiplying their natural attributes into the largest sum possible with cosmetics, clothing, and other such things.

The majority of Pym's women are not self-destructive, and they are not whiners or quitters; most of them succeed in taking what they have and creating lives that satisfy them. Though some of the characters have definite ideas about what signifies "a full life" for themselves, no underlying authorial bias suggests that a woman must work, marry, bear children, not work, not marry, or not bear children in order to live a happy and contented life. In the early novels most noticeably, but to some extent in all of them, some relatively passive women are comfortable within that style; and, from the beginning, some assertive women pursue what they want, usually in regard to men and love. Women like Agatha Hoccleve (*STG*), Helena Napier (*EW*), Allegra Gray (*EW*), and Jessie Morrow (*JP*), to name a few, act to attain what they want and win grudging admiration from their cohorts. For Pym's heroines who lack something they desire, the decision to exert themselves on their own behalf is essential; but for all of them, regardless of their style, the achievement or development of self-knowledge is vital.

In the early novels, Pym's male characters seem to be emotional ciphers. There are a few exceptions, like Ricardo Bianco (*STG*) and Francis Cleveland (*CH*), but most of the men have no significant emotions or needs. They might be vain, irritable, charming, stodgy, earnest, or self-involved, but they possess, as far as we can see, only trivial emotions, reserving their serious attention (if they are capable of it at all) for their work. Men like Henry Hoccleve (*STG*), Julian Malory (*EW*), and Nicholas Cleveland (*JP*) are amusing but foolish, childish, and ineffectual. Those who wish to marry, like Everard Bone (*EW*), seem to be motivated by practicality; those who intend to marry, like Julian Malory (*EW*) and Fabian Driver (*JP*), are outsmarted by capable women. Altogether, they cannot be taken seriously as complete people. But this dismal class gradually changes, and Pym's men become, as the result of her greater confidence in her perspective, thinking and feeling individuals not radically different from women in their problems and needs. As a class, they perhaps never become quite as attractive or capable as Pym's women, and there are still among them some silly people, like Mary Beamish's brother and Wilfred Bason (*GB*), and some superficial types, like Ned (*SDD*) and Graham Pettifer (*FGL*). Nevertheless, Pym's men in the middle and later novels are credited with minds and hearts as emotionally complex and as desirous of fulfillment as women's.

Most of Pym's major characters seek fulfillment in romantic love, but her treatment of it is often unromantic, as the commentary on the novels will demonstrate. Rather than presenting hearts throbbing as one, the author more frequently shows the false starts, errors, self-deceptions, machinations, practicalities, and failures that surround romantic love. Her essentially unromantic attitude is nowhere more evident than in her portrayal of marriage, the supposed apotheosis of lovers into the realms of permanent happiness. In Pym's world, some people prefer not to marry. Typically, the engagements or matrimonially promising relationships made in the novels spring from a woman's determination, from practical reasons, or from the deliberate decision that matrimony itself (rather than a particular person) is desirable. Marriages tend to be humdrum, boring affairs whose basis may have been love, but whose fate, at best, is tolerant companionship. Pym's novels make us conclude that those who desire romance can have it only through relationships removed from everyday reality, like Belinda Bede's (*STG*), or through serial affections and flirtations, like Harriet Bede's (STG), Prudence Bates's (*JP*), and Leonora Eyre's (*SDD*). The marriages depicted in the novels may be comfortable, cozy, affectionate, and even renewed, like Wilmet Forsyth's (*GB*), but they are just as likely to be disappointing, irritating, or unfulfilling. They are of course a form of the vital connectedness that has so many guises, but they are not romantic.

There is no focused sexuality in Pym's novels, which deal, instead, with sentimental love. We assume that all the married couples sleep together, and we know that Catherine and Tom (*LTA*), Piers and Keith (*GB*), James and Phoebe (*SDD*), James and Ned (*SDD*), and Emma and Graham (*FGL*) have sexual relationships. There are dark hints that Jessie and Fabian (*JP*) do, too. However, physical passion is attributed only to James and Ned, and Pym just indicates it before dissolving the pertinent scene with a discreet fade-out. Her unemphatic treatment of sexual love is consistent with her typically reticent characters; additionally, it circumvents the confusion of sex and love to suggest that love is the key issue, and that it takes many forms. Sexual love may be of greater interest to the modern reader than the affections for family, friends, or pets, but in Pym's world it is not intrinsically better. There is no doubt that physical passion is a vital aspect of mature, fulfilled love, but Pym's typical subject is not such love; it is the choice to extend the isolated self into relationship with the world through any one of the forms of affection. Pym's protagonists must recognize or fail to recognize their need for love, and they must choose to satisfy or to ignore that need. This being an imperfect world, the conventional versions of emotional fulfillment may be unattainable, but such deficiencies, Pym's novels suggest, can be filled by other options for gratifying the universal need to love.

In Pym's exploration of her subject, five topics recur, gathering increasing power and depth with each subsequent treatment: the need for love, the definition of emotional purpose from the needs of others, observation versus participation, the impact of the imagination on the emotional life, and unsuitable attachments or love objects. My commentary will focus on the relevance of these topics to the novels as I consider each in turn, but an overview will indicate the scope of our context.

Pym's emphasis on the need for love reflects the conviction that emotional isolation—which is sometimes a temptation, other times an unrecognized condition—has drastic effects on individual lives. It might seem unnecessary to single it out as one of her major themes because most of her characters acknowledge, or act as if they have, a need to connect with others emotionally. But some do not. At first most of those who deny or seem to lack this need are men, but eventually women are shown to share the problem. As I have already suggested, the need for love in Pym's novels can take many forms and find many outlets. The use of the word *love* to describe relationships besides the romantic or familial ones is justified, if it needs justification, by the novels themselves. They suggest that the desire for emotional closeness, the need for companionship, the wish to belong, to be with others who have common values, points of view, and contexts, may be satisfied by lovers, relatives, friends, or fellow members of a community. The implied importance of community to all her characters becomes explicit in *Quartet in Autumn*, in which Pym articulates its significance fully. Underlying the concept of community is an essential form of love, an attitude composed of goodwill and compassion for others simply because they are fellow human beings; it is the responsible benevolence toward others enjoined by the commandment to "Love thy neighbor as thyself." Paraphrasing Piers Longridge (*GB*), we might say that such love is the recognition that we are all colleagues in the business of getting through life. But, descending to a humbler level, the need for companionship and the expression of self may be satisfied also in a relationship with a pet, so Pym's emphasis on the multiple possibilities suggests a corollary to the need for love: options for emotional fulfillment.

The definition of emotional purpose from the needs of others may apply to any kind of love that includes responsibility or responsiveness to a perceived weakness. Many of Pym's characters need to feel needed or wish to make a difference to someone. Looking to others enables a person so motivated to find his niche, to define himself as someone having a purpose vis-à-vis other living beings. Wilmet Forsyth pursues Piers (*GB*) because she believes he needs her help. Rupert Stonebird sees Penelope Grandison (*UA*) as a vulnerable person—her efforts to enhance her attractiveness so often go awry—and wishes to confirm the desirability she tries to create. Daphne Dagnall (*FGL*) and Winifred Malory (*EW*) feel it is their duty to make homes for their unmarried brothers, and all of Pym's male and female do-gooders are moved by a similar sense of responsibility toward others. Mrs. Beltane (*NFR*) and Liz (*SDD*) are responsible for animals, to which their care is imperative. And even Tom Mallow worries because he wants to *matter* somehow. Since he identifies himself so entirely with his work, he expresses his concern as the fear that his studies will benefit or make a difference to no one, but he, too, feels the need for an emotional purpose.

The conflict or distinction between observation and participation represents a person's characteristic orientation toward life, and involves his view of himself, others, and himself in relation to others. The difference is between a positive, life-affirming stance from which a character perceives himself as part of his world, with all its potential problems and difficulties, and a distant, judgmental stance from which he perceives himself as alien to his community and uninvolved with its concerns. Sometimes, Pym combines observation with a participatory spirit to give us characters who are unhappy about their lives. Mildred Lathbury (*EW*), who seems so involved with people, feels like an observer because her own feelings are not primary to herself. Alaric Lydgate's observation of others indicates his loneliness and an interest in others akin to Rhoda Wellcome's

(*LTA*). But sometimes observation combines with detachment, as in Tom Mallow, and then it signals a life-denying alienation. Though Pym often amuses us with snoopy people watching others from convenient windows, the person who is only an observer is an unfortunate.

The lively minds of most of Pym's major characters enable her to explore several aspects of the imagination. She presents it as a supplement to the emotional life, in people like Belinda Bede and Prudence Bates. But imagination has the power also to shape the self and others, and these capacities, especially, figure in Pym's analysis of romantic love. Although some people, like Belinda, Jessie Morrow (*JP*), and Dulcie Mainwaring (*NFR*), see their loves relatively clearly, most of Pym's characters do not. Instead, they fall in love with images of their own creation and with images of themselves whose reflections they see in their lovers' eyes. On a larger scale, Pym suggests that the imaginative creation of selves and others is a common activity, and the most interesting instance she gives us is in *Jane and Prudence*, whose women join to create Man, a remarkable being.

The subject of unsuitable attachments or love objects comes up so often in these novels that one might imagine Pym's people falling in love with leggy chorus girls or mustachioed reprobates. They do not go this far, but they do love others who are conventionally inappropriate choices, and that theme represents the conflict between the individual and society, between emotion and propriety. Through this subject, Pym treats the public intrusion into the private situation, conventionality—the more potent because Pym's characters value it so highly. It is a frequent concern because she gives full value to the social or moral values or inhibitions that make her characters the solid, decent people they are. As the novels progress, we understand the relative nature of concepts of suitability.

In Pym's world, there is no such thing as an unsuitable attachment, though the characters think often enough in standard terms of class, education, and age. Even the most careful guardians against scandal or breaches of the social code distinguish between loving and expressing the emotion. Implicitly, the consensus is that loving someone—

anyone—cannot be wrong; however, showing such love in what is considered an improper fashion is something else. But even within the restrictions imposed by the moral or social codes they accept, most of Pym's characters find satisfying ways of expressing their feelings. Besides, truly scandalous behavior never tempts many people in Pym's world because their own restraint and decency makes them adequate judges of what is suitable or unsuitable behavior. In fact, for some the necessity is to overcome the senseless prohibitions imposed by their own esteem for conventionality. Finally, from the reader's point of view, the only unsuitable attachments in these novels are those devoid of affection or those motivated by purely self-enhancing reasons, such as the wish to feel superior, the need to prove one's power to attract others, or the desire to possess someone. However, even these are "unsuitable" only as regards the self-centered person; if the partner in the relationship is moved by love, the attachment cannot be unsuitable for him, although we might consider it unsatisfactory or unfortunate. There is, in Pym's world, no love that is unsuitable.

II. EXCELLENT AND LESS EXCELLENT WOMEN

Barbara Pym's first four novels (including one unpublished during her life) establish the thematic concerns whose exploration in depth was to be her primary concern as a novelist. *Some Tame Gazelle* focuses particularly on unsuitable love objects and a variety of options for emotional fulfillment; *Crampton Hodnet* also treats unsuitable attachments and emphasizes the need for love; *Excellent Women* features a heroine torn between observation or participation in the life of feeling, who defines her emotional purpose from the needs of others; and *Jane and Prudence* especially examines the impact of the imagination on the emotional lives of its two main characters. The author's treatment of love is acute and insightful from the beginning, and her vision achieves a special piquancy by her mastery of comedy. Fiction that reveals the underlying, essential needs beneath what is often remarkable and foolish behavior is obviously serious business, but Pym's work persuades us that it need not be somber or solemn. We laugh at characters like Belinda Bede, but the author does not permit us to scoff at the emotions and motivations that inspire her; they are ours, too.

In these early novels, however, Pym is not certain that the emotions and motivations she writes about are "ours." She concentrates on the feminine point of view, generally, and does not venture too often or too comfortably into the inner lives of the men who interact with her women. Overall, her early characters and plots suggest that radical differences separate women and men, with women having different natures, needs, problems, and perceptions. However, the first glimpses of the insight that the complex emotional life she grants to women is universal are also in evidence, though they are set forth tentatively, in minor or incompletely realized characters. Consideration of these matters follows my observations on the first four novels, works which suggest the gradual development of the beginning novelist but also demonstrate Pym's acuity of perception.

Some Tame Gazelle features two unmarried sisters, includes two proposals, and ends with two weddings, one actual, the other anticipated. The novel treats love triangles, impossible or unrequited loves, and belated discoveries of a "preference" for someone other than a spouse. Though accurate, this synopsis of Barbara Pym's first novel is misleading. It suggests a modern variation on the traditional marriage plot (with an affair here or a divorce there to achieve hard-won insight or romantic resolution), and nothing could be further from the truth. But the synopsis uncovers the romantic materials Pym dislocates, by focusing on characters in their fifties, to remind us that love is not the exclusive property of youth, and marriage not its only goal. Indeed, *Some Tame Gazelle* develops finally as an unmarriage plot: Belinda and Harriet Bede, the recipients of the two proposals, are not the ageing stars of the weddings. When each sister confirms spinsterhood as her happiest choice, the novel suggests that while love is essential to the emotionally fulfilled life, marriage is not. The author, then, turns the staples of the romantic novel upside down: her heroine and hero are settled into late middle-age; love in their world is rarely anguished or even unsettling; marriage is not the glorious conclusion to the heroine's story, though she is given the option; and marriage itself is not the supreme love-inspired choice by which a man supposedly validates a woman's singularity or worth.

"Some tame gazelle, or some gentle dove: / Something to love, oh, something to love!" The novel's epigraph, a quotation from Thomas Haynes Bayly, indicates its main theme. Other themes, in addition to the need to love, include options for emotional fulfillment, reality versus imagination, passion versus comfortable love, happiness as a minimalist art, and, the most important in our present context, unsuitable love objects. Overt conflict in the novel develops from the introduction of outsiders into a country village so insular that everyone is as well acquainted with others' hobby-horses as with their wardrobes. Two of these outsiders seriously threaten the heroine's emotional well-being. The most obvious conflict, however, is the undeclared and more-or-less covert antagonism between Belinda and Agatha, between the archdeacon's endearingly innocent lover and his wife. Their battles rage over everything from the relative chic of the women's clothing to the arrangement of marrow squash for display. Because the conflict expresses itself primarily in Agatha's snubs, little insults well within the bounds of social acceptability, its real arena is within, in Belinda's alert mind. In addition, Pym sketches a mock-conflict between two women, one in her fifties, the other in her thirties, for the heart of a curate in his twenties.

The epigraph, one of the sentimental Belinda's favorite quotations, is opposed in the novel by another quotation: "Love is only one of many passions and it has no great influence on the sum of life." Samuel Johnson's assertion is favored by Nicholas Parnell, the school friend visiting the archdeacon. A single man, Parnell speaks for the antiromantic view of love and marriage in the novel, and his cynical perspective is confirmed by the proposals made to Belinda and her sister, and by the relationship of Henry and Agatha Hoccleve. The villagers agree that Agatha is the power behind the archdeacon and that the "Hoccleves [are] sometimes rather snappy with each other." Various degrees of exasperation characterize their feelings for each other. Once or twice a gesture of affection passes between the Hoccleves, but their union seems to be cemented especially by the habit of mutual, low-level irritation and the utter unthinkability of any option. Parnell has always felt lucky not to be "caught" by a determined woman and insists that practicality should be the basis of marriage: "the emotions of the heart are very transitory, or so I believe; I should think it makes one much happier to be well-fed than well-loved." Sixty, he remarks, is a good age for a man to marry so that a woman can "help him into his grave." His thoughts on marriage are evoked by Harriet Bede's refusal of a suitable husband in Nathaniel Mold, his deputy librarian and fellow visitor.

Harriet, Belinda's mid-fiftyish sister, is a cheerful, somewhat loud woman whose appearance is of great interest to herself:

> Harriet came into the room, radiant in flowered voile. Tropical flowers rioted over her plump body. The background was the green of the jungle, the blossoms were crimson and mauve, of an unknown species. Harriet was still attractive in a fat Teu-

tonic way. She did not wear her pince-nez when curates came to supper. (11)

Belinda's mild sense of superiority to Harriet is based in part on the latter's plumpness and vanity. Harriet is continually reinforcing the corsets she wears under her tight but fashionable clothes. Nevertheless, she attracts men, and Pym, to underline the sisters' choice to lavish their affections on conventionally unsuitable objects, gives them each appropriate admirers. Mr. Mold is one of these. His suitability seems obvious to Parnell: about the same age as Harriet, he shares her love of comfort and good food. Moreover, the financially comfortable man holds a most respectable post. From Harriet's point of view, his jovial manner and distinguished appearance (in a rosy, stocky sort of way) are important as well. She does not notice the occasional, nearly imperceptible coarseness of manner and speech that reminds the finicky Belinda of his "low origin."

Mold knows a suitable wife for a librarian when he sees one and decides, on the strength of two meetings, to propose. There is no courtship whatever, except the mild ogling and flirtation that enliven an after-church chat and a dinner party. Indeed, so little does Mr. Mold know Harriet that he arrives at the Bedes' house the morning after the dinner ready to propose—unless she does not look good in daylight. Though she is perhaps too heavily powdered, Harriet passes the sunshine test, and Mold begins his proposal with the remarkable observation that they have "so much in common":

> Encouraged by her silence Mr. Mold went on: "What I mean to say is, that I think we should be very happy if we married. My house is large and comfortable and my financial position is sound . . . and," he added, rather as an afterthought, "I loved you the moment I saw you." (137)

Harriet, remembering the dowdy coat she wore on their first meeting, thinks about the proverbial blindness of love. She overlooks the afterthought quality of his final declaration, but even her robust vanity cannot overlook the "prosaic and casual" aspect of the proposal: Mr. Mold did not "sound as if he really *cared* at all." He does not. His offer is motivated entirely by Harriet's suitability as a wife "for the deputy Librarian of one of England's greatest libraries," and he leaves the village repeating Parnell's favorite quotation.

Harriet is a severe judge of proposals thanks to Count Ricardo Bianco, another eminently suitable man who is in the habit of asking her, from time to time, to be his wife. The count sets the standard when it comes to proposals. He kneels, pleads, grows pale, and quotes "the greater Italian poets." Ricardo has everything to recommend him to a romantic taste. An Italian gentleman of a generous and melancholy nature, he has style, beautiful manners, and money. The fortunate Harriet, his beloved Laura, rejects him as regularly as he offers himself. An obvious contrast to Mr. Mold, Ricardo does not worship Harriet because of her suitability; in fact, Agatha remarks several times that Lady Clara Boulding, the widow of a member of Parliament, should be his logical choice. In spite of this, Ricardo's heart belongs to Harriet. Its youthful ardor is touching, except, apparently, to his *belle dame sans merci*: he has only to see Harriet to gush ecstatic compliments; he attends church only because it might bring him closer to her, and sits at a good vantage point for gazing at her; he is made more than usually melancholy by Harriet's attention to other men; and he suffers terribly from the rumors that she is to marry Mr. Mold. But Harriet, though she enjoys his adulation and proposals tremendously, is immovable.

In the novel (as so often in life) the flashy woman attracts more admirers than her less colorful sister: Pym gives Harriet two would-be husbands, Belinda only one. The heroine of *Some Tame Gazelle* wears shapeless dresses, sensible shoes, and woollies. She would certainly laugh at a comparison with Alexander Pope's Belinda, but if she thought of it, she might acknowledge that her own quiet circle demonstrates "What dire offence from amorous causes springs, / What mighty contests rise from trivial things." In her late fifties, Belinda feels she is poor, substandard heroine material:

> Once, she knew, she *had* been different, and perhaps after all the years had left her with a little of that difference. Perhaps she was still an original shining like a comet, mingling no water with her wine. But only very occasionally, mostly she was just like everyone else, rather less efficient, if anything. (28–29)

Only affectionate hyperbole could liken her to a shining comet, but an original she certainly is. She sees others as clearly and critically as she sees herself because she cannot help being acute; yet she also sees and treats them with kindliness because she has a compassionate heart. Belinda's combination of perception and manner apprises us of the real distinction between a sociable generosity and ordinary social hypocrisy. However, her generosity fails her when it comes to Theo Grote, bishop of Mbawawa.

From the moment the bishop arrives for a visit at the vicarage, he singles out the amazed Belinda. She is astonished, first of all, because the good-looking young curate she remembers has evolved into this yellow, stringy prelate who reminds her first of a sheep and later of a fish. Moreover, Theo had been, in their youth, one of Harriet's beaux—but he now believes it was Belinda who knitted him a beautiful scarf and expressed a great interest in missions. Her protestations of innocence avail her nothing. He does not remember Harriet at all, and soon dismisses her from his mind as "an extremely silly woman." Belinda, no less than her sister, had anticipated the renewal of Theo's courtship of Harriet; instead, the two or three expressive glances a bishop may permit himself land unmistakably on Belinda.

A bishop, even a bishop of Mbawawa, is a very good catch by village standards, but Belinda is not impressed. If anything, she feels that peculiar annoyance women reserve for unwelcome suitors. Unfairly, the bishop's fish-and-sheepish attentions seem to Belinda to reflect unfavorably on herself and, naturally, she dislikes them (and him) all the more. The crisis comes on a day when she is dishevelled and floury, making ravioli from the count's recipe. Obviously, Theo did not become a bishop by wasting time. Within moments of being admitted into the Bedes' drawing room, he remarks that Belinda has probably noticed his preference for her "above all the other ladies of the village." She denies this charge with alacrity and hastens to inform him, catching his drift and trying to deflect him, that she is not special. He agrees. Justifiably, Belinda is miffed by the assertion that "She is not fair to outward view"; understandably, she is irked by the reminder that she is not used to offers of marriage. But when Theo alludes to *Paradise Lost*, it is more than mortal flesh can bear:

> Belinda interrupted him with a startled exclamation. "*Paradise Lost!*" she echoed in horror. "*Milton. . . .*"
>
> "I think when one has reached er—riper years," the Bishop continued, "things are different, aren't they?" . . .
>
> "I'm afraid I can't marry you," she said, looking down at her floury hands. "I don't love you."
>
> "But you respect and like me," said the Bishop, as if that went without saying. "We need not speak of love—one would hardly expect that now." (224)

The bishop's proposal to Belinda is even more prosaic than Mr. Mold's to Harriet because the deputy librarian pretended at least that love dictated his offer. Perhaps Theo feels compelled to honesty by his position in the Church. He agrees with the view of Parnell and Mold that, past a certain age, romantic love is no longer a factor in marriage or even in the emotional life of a reasonable person.

Pym does not permit us to believe that Theo shares our partiality, based on her character and personality, for Belinda. When she declines the honor he offers her, he assures her that he will not give it another thought. The truthfulness of this assurance is evident in his department-store proposal to Connie Aspinall. We can assume that Edith Liversidge's poor relation shares Theo's practical view. Connie's overriding concern with social status, evident in her fond memories of her life with Lady Grudge in Belgrave Square, her financial dependence, and her love of titles, accounts for her acceptance of the determined bishop. The reader can only agree with Belinda that it is "manifest" that "God moves in a mysterious way."

Harriet cannot marry Mr. Mold or the count because her heart is given to curates. Her long-standing fondness for these young men is important in the muted sisterly rivalry between her and Belinda. The novel opens with the sisters' supper for Mr. Donne, and ends at his wedding reception with Harriet's supper invitation to the curate who will replace him—in her heart as well as in the parish. There have been many others before Mr. Donne, and there will be others after his successor, young men in their twenties for her to coddle happily. Belinda feels these serial affections are not quite suitable, inferior, certainly, to her own ancient affection for the riper Henry.

Since the sisters guess Mr. Donne to be about twenty-three or twenty-four, the discrepancy between his age and Harriet's might suggest a motherly attachment on her part. But this is not entirely accurate. Not that there is the slightest hint of impropriety in Harriet's behavior, but her attitude is more romantic than motherly. Calling on Mr. Donne in mid-afternoon, for example, she imagines defiantly that she is observed from behind twitching curtains and that she will be the object of gossip—quite as if she were keeping a clandestine assignation. The visit itself is "disappointing," though her gifts of food and her offer of hand-knitted socks are gratefully received, because she hears of another woman with willing needles: "This Olivia Berridge knitting socks for him, that was the trouble." Harriet is slightly mollified to learn that her competitor is "a kind of female Don," but wastes no time in finding out what she can about her, especially her age (about thirty). Later, when the sisters hear the false story that Donne is engaged to her, the brazen Harriet forces him to say he sees Olivia "as an elder sister." But in the long run, she fights a losing battle. Olivia, whose age observation amends to "the early or middle thirties," proposes to Donne. On hearing the news from Agatha Hoccleve, who encouraged her niece to make the offer, Belinda frets about Harriet: "Not that one could say it had really been a 'disappointment' to Harriet in the usual sense, but what would she do without a curate to dote upon?" Fortunately, she does not have to wait long before "another had come in [Donne's] place, so like, that they would hardly realize the difference, except he was rather Italian-looking and had had a nervous breakdown."

Just as Harriet does not look to young men from a lack of more suitable choices, neither, obviously, does Belinda focus on Henry Hoccleve because there is no one else. She might have had Theodore Mbawawa, after all. Few of us, probably, can think of a situation more intrinsically horrible than Belinda's: the nightmarish idea of being stuck forever on the adored youth who rejected our girlish love is too terrible for words. But that is precisely Belinda's situation:

Belinda, having loved the Archdeacon when she was twenty and not having found anyone to replace him since, had naturally got into the habit of loving him, though with the years her passion had mellowed into a comfortable feeling, more like the cosiness of a winter evening by the fire than the uncertain rapture of a spring morning. (17)

Clearly, Ricardo's habit of loving Harriet, and Harriet's of loving curates, are related to Belinda's habit of loving Henry. It is hard to understand why Belinda's love did not wither when Henry married Agatha. Several times, she expresses a real fear of rejection and change, so perhaps it was less threatening for her, after Henry's marriage, not to chance another failure. He has forgotten how boring he used to find Belinda's adulation, but she has not forgotten the pain she suffered when he married. Still, Pym makes it sound vaguely comical, as if Belinda's lazy heart just never got around (in thirty-odd years) to replacing Henry with another man. The pain, after all, is a memory, and her present feeling is a cozy one, "like a warm comfortable garment, bedsocks, perhaps, or even woollen combinations."

Initially, Belinda's love of Henry might seem foolish, but it is a more clearsighted affection than we might expect. She is under very few illusions about his character. Even if he were not patently the archdeacon married to the redoubtable and eternal Agatha, he might still seem an unsuitable object for her love. "Dear Henry" is all ego and Belinda knows it. Marvelously pompous and vain, he enjoys assuming preoccupied poses among the monuments in the churchyard. He loves to read aloud, especially from seventeenth-century authors. His congregation, denied by tradition the mid-sermon use of legs or hasty excuses, is usually his audience. But Belinda loves to hear him read—and to look at him, since "The years had dealt kindly with him and he had grown neither bald nor fat." Henry seems eccentric to the vicarage servants because he has "a hankering after the picturesque and would have liked a ha-ha, a ruined temple, grottoes, waterfalls and gloomily overhanging trees" in his garden. But the archdeacon resorts to the churchyard precisely because he is deprived of a more imaginative setting for the image he cultivates of eighteenth-century melancholia. More than anything else, the self-centered and sometimes querulous hero of Belinda's heart wants admiration; consequently, he envies the attentions paid to Mr. Donne or Mr. Plowman, the other clergymen in the village. He chortles at the discomfort awaiting Theo Grote in the vicarage guestroom, taking special pleasure in locking up his collection of murder mysteries and leaving Theo an Icelandic grammar for night reading. Henry is not at all selfless, and is entertaining in a peevish, self-dramatizing fashion. Though she frequently tries to excuse his failings, Belinda is not blind to Henry's faults or affectations.

For the present, loving Henry means nothing more threatening or demanding for Belinda than paying admiring attention to him, wearing blue (because he expressed a preference for it many years ago), being loyal to him when he is criticized by Harriet or others, and thinking about him fondly all the time when she is not actually in his presence. Wonderfully, Belinda feels no bitterness in her love. As Pym presents it, her love, though largely unrequited, is a positive gain because it gives her an emotional focal point and, just as importantly, links her to others. One day, for example, after she remarks to herself that Miss Jenner, who runs the wool shop, is foolish about traveling salesmen, her thought develops uncomfortably: "And perhaps we are all silly over something or somebody without knowing it; perhaps her own behaviour with the Archdeacon was no less silly than Miss Jenner's with the travellers." Belinda dismisses the idea, but her sense of connectedness recurs with a Ricardo dejected by Harriet's seeming infatuation with Mr. Mold. Belinda exhorts him not to lose hope and offers the thought that "it is better to have loved and lost than never to have loved at all." Perhaps because he is Italian, Ricardo does not dismiss her statement as a cliché but acknowledges it as a comforting truth: "'You are so kind and understanding,' he said. 'I feel that there is a great bond between us.'" Belinda's love for Henry fosters her bond with others.

Belinda's great opportunity comes when Agatha goes on a month-long vacation to Karlsbad. She envisions the daring possibility of inviting Henry for meals without having to include his wife. Soon after Agatha departs, Henry drops in on the sisters, and Belinda is given the opportunity to mend one of his socks. It proves to be "an upsetting and unnerving experience," especially because the last time she saw Agatha, the latter had been busy with the same wifely task. But some of her pleasure in having Henry all to herself is diluted by worrying continually what others will say, and even the absent wife inhibits Belinda in her innocent expressions of love. When, for instance, the sight of some clerical gray wool inspires her to knit Henry a sweater, she goes so far as to buy it. But even before she leaves the shop, she knows it will never be done. When we grow older we lack the fine courage of youth, and even an ordinary task like making a pullover for somebody we love or used to love seems too dangerous to be undertaken. Then Agatha might get to hear of it; that was something else to be considered. Her long, thin fingers might pick at it critically and detect a mistake in the ribbing at the Vee neck; there was often some difficulty there. (83) Still, she appropriates the exasperation Agatha would have felt at Henry's continual idleness and scolds him for sitting on a damp seat in the churchyard. "It was just the kind of remark that Agatha would make," Henry thinks. That, of course, is what makes it so delicious a moment for Belinda.

One of the high points for Belinda of the Agatha-free month is Henry's impromptu invitation to tea. She does not accept it. Too considerate to keep her sister waiting, Belinda rushes home, pitifully aware that she might have missed a "once in a lifetime" treat. But her serene disappointment brings her an important insight: "Of course, there was a certain pleasure in not doing something; it was impossible that one's high expectations should be disappointed by reality." Belinda's preference for imaginary pleasures is the accommodation of a happy temperament to an irreversible situation, but even when the real emotional climax comes she recognizes how essential to her feeling is its distance from the wear-and-tear of reality. After tea at the vicarage, Harriet and Nicholas Parnell depart with some haste before Henry starts reading aloud. Belinda listens contentedly for one solid hour and is rewarded by hearing, finally, the declaration that makes it all worthwhile.

> "Florrie never bothers to dust my study when Agatha's away," said the Archdeacon, seeing where Belinda was looking.
> "No, things always go wrong in a house when there's no woman at the head of things," agreed Belinda. "I mean, it's

different when Agatha's away."

    The Archdeacon sighed. "Yes, it is different," he agreed.
"But there it is. We can't alter things, can we?" (150–51)

The elated Belinda stays to supper with Henry and Parnell,
reliving the past so successfully that she goes home thoroughly happy. She means to say nothing to Harriet, but
Ovaltine loosens her tongue and she shares "the moment
[she's] been waiting for for thirty years" with her sister. In
the afterglow of her romantic moment, Belinda reflects that
all it takes to be happy is "Just one evening like that every
thirty years or so." Clearly, she has won mastery over happiness as a minimalist art. What excessive pathos there
might seem to be in this tremulous delight over a scrap is
modified by Belinda's own perception: "Possibly . . . I love
him even more than Agatha does, but my feeling may be the
stronger for not having married him."

    Henry's vague hint that he now prefers Belinda to Agatha
is not enough to equalize the combat between the two
women. Besides, Belinda's own sympathy for her rival keeps
intruding itself, as when she realizes that a month away
from the archdeacon has done wonders for Agatha's looks.
But finally she learns two things about her well-dressed
nemesis that make her easier to deal with. When Agatha almost admits that Olivia Berridge proposed to Donne, she
adds that women often do this, men being "shy about offering what seems to them very little":

> At this moment an idea came into Belinda's head. At first it
> seemed fantastic, then quite likely, and finally almost a cer-
> tainty. Agatha had proposed to Henry. Why had this never
> occurred to her before? And now that it had, what was the use
> of it? Belinda could not answer this, but she knew that she
> could put it away in her mind and take it out again when she
> was feeling in need of comfort. (216)

To top it off, when Belinda remarks that she would never
dream of proposing to a man herself, in case that "one met
somebody else afterwards"—this from the woman who has
loved Henry all these years—Agatha's face softens and she
responds, "One wonders how often it *does* happen when
one knows that it *can*." Thus Belinda concludes that Agatha
has recently discovered in herself a preference for Theo

26

Grote. All the signs are there: Agatha thinks the stiff and leathery bishop "kind and amusing," flushes when she speaks of him, and beams at him happily every chance she gets (she is not otherwise a beamer). But the decisive pieces of evidence are the socks she knits for him, socks whose defect ("not quite long enough in the foot") Theo ungallantly reports to Belinda. It is almost too much for the compassionate Belinda, who feels "she could almost love Agatha as a sister now."

In fact, Belinda's contentment with the status quo derives in large part from already having a sister. Her only serious anxiety in the course of the novel is that the unpredictable Harriet might choose to marry Mr. Mold or Theo Grote. This tolerant and loving relationship with its stability, familiarity, and companionable sharing is central to the sisters, though Belinda recognizes its importance more clearly than Harriet. In her relationship with her bossy and sometimes intimidating sister, her needs for affection and intimacy are satisfied. To her, the proposals she and Harriet survive represent the evils of change safely averted. The sisters' relationship, as Pym presents it, is a satisfactory alternative to the male-female relationship conventionally accepted as being primary. Unquestionably, Belinda and Harriet are happier with each other than they would be with the bishop and Mr. Mold. In a better world, perhaps Belinda would have married Henry. But things being as they are, she and Harriet have an option that enables them to express their loving natures, to fulfill their needs to love and be loved in return.

The men chosen by the sisters as romantic objects suggest that neither marriage nor the "suitability" of an individual is essential when it comes to love. Ricardo Bianco, as we remarked earlier, is eligible and romantically impeccable. Despite Harriet's continued refusal to marry him, the count continues to ask her because he continues to love her; and Harriet will not marry him because, though she is fond of him, she does not love him. If merely being married or being loved were the point, Harriet would certainly marry her ardent Italian, but in this novel, it is more blessed to give than to receive. Belinda knows she and Harriet can get along without the two outsiders because she knows that by rejecting marriage they still have the satisfying sentimental attachments that in no way threaten their comfortable and affectionate life with each other. Since they can have their cake and nibble from another—and since this arrangement satisfies them—why should the Bede sisters marry?

Considered as a whole, the characters' attachments form a zany chain. Agatha prefers the bishop; the bishop (though he eventually marries Connie Aspinall) prefers Belinda; Belinda loves the archdeacon; and Henry, safely married to Agatha, safely hints that he prefers Belinda, and loves himself. But despite all of these unsuitable attachments, no ripples appear on the calm surface of the village. In Belinda's world, love or a preference for someone is expressed by listening to and indulging him, responding to a beauty of person or character that others fail to perceive, giving little presents, or knitting for him—hardly scandalous material. Romantic love is defined by the novel as a desire to *give* to the particular someone who gladdens the heart and eye, a need to act and feel in regard *to* someone. From the conventional view of fulfillment, a chaste love for a permanently married man, for someone other than one's unchangeable spouse, or for an absurdly young curate is unsuitable, to be sure. But Pym persuades us that these attachments are valid and valuable expressions of a very basic need. The unromantic but essential truth occurs to Belinda as she reflects on the new curate who is to replace Donne: "Some tame gazelle or some gentle dove or even a poodle dog—something to *love*, that was the point." Archdeacon or gazelle, sister or dove, curate or bishop or poodle: the particular object of affection is immaterial, so long as there is an object. Parnell's quotation from Samuel Johnson is refuted resoundingly by Harriet and Belinda's refusal, for love's sake, of the proposals made them, and by the importance of their sisterly love for each other.

Crampton Hodnet

One of the chapters of *Crampton Hodnet* is entitled "An Unexpected Outcome," and such a criticism might be made about the book as a whole. Pym wrote the novel in 1939–1940 after she had finished the first draft of *Some Tame Gazelle*. She did not revise the manuscript for a publisher's consideration. After her death, her friend and literary executor, Hazel Holt, undertook its revision—"based," according to the book jacket, "on pencilled revisions made by the author and knowledge gained through long editorial collaboration with her." Though the book has some good "bits," as Pym remarked, it also has several flaws. The novel itself and Pym's subsequent use, in *Jane and Prudence*, of Jessie Morrow and Miss Doggett suggest that she salvaged them from apprentice work she left unfinished. My remarks will be correspondingly brief.

Overplotting accounts for the novel's unexpected outcome. There are two story lines here. Both are interesting on their own, but their failure to interact significantly creates a sense of thinness and a lack of focus. Rather than a satisfying intertwining, the author gives us separate plots, mirror images with the potential to enrich by lending insight to each other: Stephen Latimer, a discouraged and beleaguered young man, fears passion and tries to escape (via an unsuitable attachment) into safe and cozy affection. But Jessie rejects his proposal and later he falls in love with someone else. Francis Cleveland, bored and dissatisfied in his middle age, yearns for passion and tries to escape (through an unsuitable attachment) the cozy tedium of marriage. But Barbara Bird rejects him and he goes back, chastised, to his wife. Both plots center, in a way, on unsuitable attachments and on the opposition of emotional disengagement to passionate romantic love. But the parallel plots do not finally illuminate each other in a meaningful way. For Pym, who found her métier in the combination of detailed characterization and mundane incident, *Crampton Hodnet* includes too many characters, too many—and some too ominous—episodes. Events such as the wet walk that leads Jessie Morrow and Stephen Latimer to share the secret of "Crampton Hodnet" receive disproportionate attention since little use is made of them for plot development or complication.

Initially, Miss Doggett, an aged Oxford busybody, and Jessie, her companion, seem to be the central characters. The combination of the satirical Jessie with the self-important Miss Doggett, who tries to monopolize Stephen and the undergraduates she entertains for tea, produces some fine comedy. But Pym does not make Latimer, one of her good-looking and coddled curates, convincing. In midnovel, his character changes drastically and without apparent motivation. After his unbelievable and unsuitable proposal to the plain spinster, he, Jessie, and Miss Doggett recede into the background. Other characters, like Althea Cleveland and Simon Beddoes, also introduced as if they were going to figure importantly, almost disappear from the plot. Subsequently, the novel concentrates almost exclusively on the relationship of Francis Cleveland and Barbara Bird (who appears, though greatly changed, in *Jane and Prudence*).

There are some uncharacteristic touches of gloom and bitterness in *Crampton Hodnet*. Stephen, for instance, is cynical and disheartened about his vocation, Jessie self-pitying about her nonperson status as a companion in a stifling environment. While these deep notes seem misplaced in the petty world of North Oxford, they suggest the author's early interest in the somber perspective she would explore so successfully later, in *The Sweet Dove Died* and *Quartet in Autumn*. Perhaps the greatest surprise, from our present perspective, is that Pym centers her point of view so often on Francis Cleveland, a fellow of Randolph College at Oxford, and a lecturer in English literature. In his fifties, Francis has been made superfluous in his own home by the longevity of his marriage. He returns the compliment with his lukewarm feelings about his wife, Margaret. The second half of the novel is about his hunger for romantic love and its evanescence, its fleeting nature in general. Consequently, the almost-thirty-year marriage of the Clevelands is the off-center and blandly unsatisfactory relationship that pushes Francis into an unsuitable attachment, the insipid romance with his student, Barbara.

Typically, Pym is remarkably sympathetic to her women characters regardless of their failures or of what accommodations they make with their emotional needs. Not so with Margaret Cleveland. She is remarkably unappealing and unsympathetic, the stereotyped wife of the old-fashioned women's magazines—the woman in danger of losing her man because she no longer troubles to make herself attractive. Tactfully, those magazines implied that such carelessness could only be the result of too much time and energy expended on house or children. (It was unthinkable, apparently, that some women might not wish to allure a man who had perhaps irritated them for years, that some might not wish to expend energy trying to attract the attention of someone who was not looking anyhow, or that some simply might not care to make themselves "desirable.") Pym denies Margaret the tactful excuse of pressing interests or pursuits. She is busy, though:

> After the first year or two of married life one no longer wanted to have [a husband] continually about the house. Mrs. Cleveland hardly noticed now whether her husband was there or not, and she was too busy doing other things ever to stop and ask herself whether she was not perhaps missing something. The best she could say of Francis was that he gave her no trouble, and she thought that that was a great deal more than could be said of many husbands. (37)

Since she is as bored with Francis as he is with her, the idea of making herself appealing to him never occurs to her. She can hardly believe now that she was once in love with her somewhat lazy and pettish husband. Most of the time, they treat each other with indifference or a lazy conjugal irritation, and Margaret literally drives Francis out of the house because she dislikes having him underfoot.

In this creaky domestic archetype, driving a man out of the house means driving him into the arms of the other woman. Francis, suffering a midlife crisis, is out to punish his family, Pym suggests: "He felt angry and defiant, and bitter against his family for their neglect." He would show them, he gloats, before setting off for the ill-fated Parisian vacation with Barbara, "that he was something more than a doddering old man whose head had been turned by the admiration of a pretty young woman." Pym does not make Margaret's neglect wholly responsible; Francis deliberately uses it as his excuse to do what his aggrieved vanity will do anyhow. But his developing relationship with Barbara is pathetically ineffective as a swipe at his wife. When she is finally forced by others to take notice of it, she is determined not to discuss it with him, not to take it seriously, not to react. At a critical point, she goes off to London for a few days' shopping with her daughter.

Barbara, who does turn Francis's head, is the most laughable "other woman" imaginable. She thrills only tepidly to his advances. While they share a yen for romance, it is understandable that the idea of precisely what romance involves differs for a man in his fifties and a girl of twenty who is an idealistic "cold fish." She desires never-ending talk, quotations from seventeenth-century love poems, sighs, deep looks, and little physical contact (she tried kissing once and did not like it). Francis wants attention and the other ordinary things one might reasonably expect from a love affair. Some amusing moments develop from the couple's mismatched expectations, especially when they foresee their abortive trip to Paris. Pym is at her best later when Barbara, in a bedtime panic in the room she is sharing with Francis, flees for her platonic life, convincing herself that it is not flight but noble "renunciation." Francis easily persuades himself of his virtue in getting no further than Dover. He returns with a homely cold to Margaret, during a household crisis that enables her to keep up the pretense that nothing has happened. She does not acknowledge his return because it would mean acknowledging his defection. There is something frightening in the image of a docile Francis lying in bed while Margaret refuses to let him talk, bustling above him with thermometers and hot-water bottles: "There was nothing Mrs. Cleveland liked better than looking after an invalid."

Writing about extramarital attractions later in *Excellent Women*, *A Few Green Leaves*, and (most notably) *A Glass of Blessings*, Pym exercised delightful tact in turning potential melodrama to comic account. But in *Crampton Hodnet*, she slips into the clichés inherent in the situation. Moreover, the novel fails to establish a clear tone, so that the pathos, for instance, of Francis acknowledging the end of his emotional manhood is almost entirely lost in the novel's uneasy mixture of attitudes. We long for more insight into Margaret as she refuses to hear and then hears unwillingly about her husband's romantic involvement, but she remains too vague to enlist our interest or sympathy. Finally, notwithstanding Jessie Morrow, Miss Doggett, and its good bits, the novel is not top-notch Pym. Had the author thoroughly revised the book herself, rather than storing it for forty years, *Crampton Hodnet* might have ranked as one of her artistically cohesive and entertaining communities. As it is, it does not come up to the high standard that Pym's other novels lead us to expect.

Excellent Women

To the consternation of some and the amusement of others attending a London Lenten service in *Excellent Women*, a country parson preaches an "abusive" sermon on the Judgment Day. The elderly preacher, "of a handsome and dignified appearance" with a "strong and dramatic voice," is Belinda's Henry Hoccleve. The second novel Pym published, like the first, features a few unsuitable attachments, but emphasizes other themes: the burden of involvement, passivity versus self-determination, the onus of rejection, and, most importantly, the needs of others as emotional purpose, and observation versus participation. All of these topics center on the character and fortunes of Mildred Lathbury: *Excellent Women* is about identity as the heroine struggles with the conflict of whether she will be an excellent woman, observing the lives of others, or a woman engaged in a full life of her own.

Mildred is the narrator who denies her right, intention, or desire to be a heroine. Thirty years old, she describes herself as "mousy and rather plain"; moreover, she squelches any hope the reader might wring from that unpromising description by adding:

> I am not at all like Jane Eyre, who must have given hope to so many plain women who tell their stories in the first person, nor have I ever thought of myself as being like her. (7)

Mildred sees herself as a fussy spinster who values her own tidiness, independence, and freedom from care. The daughter of a country clergyman, she came to London after the death of her parents to live in a neighborhood that is virtually a country village within the city. The parish of St. Mary's defines Mildred's small community. She has a part-time job with an organization that helps distressed gentlewomen, an attractive apartment, a circle of friends (chief of whom are Julian, the unmarried vicar of St. Mary's, and

Winifred, his unmarried sister), and a reliable cleaning lady.

Mildred would seem to have everything, but early in the novel she remarks wistfully and naively on her inexperience with love:

> I have never been very much given to falling in love and have often felt sorry that I have so far missed not only the experience of marriage, but the perhaps even greater and more ennobling one of having loved and lost. (44)

She discounts two or three girlish crushes and nurtures no feelings for the forty-year-old Julian Malory. It is obvious that Mildred would like to marry, and that, despite her identification of herself as a spinster, she has not given up hope that it might yet happen. Since her set at St. Mary's consists of women, older men, and young boys, her phlegmatic heart, at odds with her often-felt regret, idles peacefully. It exerts itself only (but unsparingly) on the business of others: "practically anything may be the business of an unattached woman with no troubles of her own, who takes a kindly interest in those of her friends." In addition, then, to warning us about her looks and her unromantic sense of self, Mildred denies possession of the heroine's sine qua non: she has, she implies, no story of her own. The self-effacing spinster can tell a story only because it seems on the surface to be the story of others.

Mildred has the attractive quality of seeing herself with humor and some distance. If she is "mousy and rather plain," Mrs. Morris, her cleaning lady, says it is because she has not learned to "make the most" of herself. Remarkably undemanding of her friends, she is a real pushover, reliably responding to their demands on her own time. Typically, her annoyance or protests, when she has any, are thought but not uttered. She makes real but unobtrusive efforts to practice Christian charity and virtue (pains eventually rewarded with a potential husband). A likable busybody with a serious interest in the details of others' lives, Mildred is, above all, an excellent woman. This term may sound complimentary, but it is used in a somewhat patronizing way by the characters, and its gradual definition by the novel includes some qualities most of us would be loath to claim. An excellent woman, sensible, dependable, and competent at traditional womanly tasks, serves the needs of others while expecting nothing in return. She either has no important feelings of her own or passively recognizes their futility. Worthier, in many respects, than her more interesting, more assertive sisters, an excellent woman does not marry, figuring, instead, as a "rejected one." Since many of them are good churchwomen, Mildred is surrounded by others of her ilk. The confidante, the tireless helper and do-gooder, she seems content, initially, as the stalwart supporting actress in others' dramas. Mildred dispenses the tea required to get others through their crises.

Three newcomers, all of whom take for granted their starring roles, arrive to disquiet Mildred's placid life. She suspects Allegra Gray, the young and good-looking widow of a clergyman, of changing her first name (like many another star) from "a more conventional and uninteresting one." From the moment Allegra rents some spare rooms at the vicarage (space rejected by our independent heroine), she vamps Julian and displaces Mildred as Winifred Malory's favorite friend. The widow is definitely not an excellent woman, as Mildred discovers when she and Winifred are put to work hemming her curtains. "Allegra's the sort of person people *want* to give things to," Winifred gushes, explaining the widow's acquisition of a hearth rug from the vicar and a pot of jam from Father Greatorex, his curate. Julian is soon engaged to the designing woman, though the innocent Winifred and Mildred had assumed he foresaw a celibate life. The engagement is an outrage to Mrs. Morris, who considers Allegra "a pretty face": "You've done too much for Father Malory and so has Miss Winifred and in the end you both get left, if you'll excuse me putting it plainly."

Allegra, Julian, and the entire parish insist on seeing Mildred as "the rejected one," ignoring her truthful protestations that she never loved the vicar. Assuming that excellent women exist to serve her needs, Allegra adds insult to insult. She suggests that, since Winifred's housekeeping usefulness to Julian will be at an end when he marries, Mildred should give the vicar's sister a home. Obviously, the two rejected but excellent women would make ideal companions for each other. The shocked Mildred disagrees. But the lesson of Allegra's success is not lost on her, and contributes to her growing dissaffection with her role. She despairs of coloring her complexion as artfully as Allegra does hers, but buys a tube of "Hawaiian Fire" lipstick despite a saleswoman's effort to sell her "Sea Coral"—"quite pale, you know." Notwithstanding the assumptions of Julian and his apricot-faced fiancée, Mildred does not intend to languish in eternal excellent-womanhood.

Helena and Rocky Napier move into the flat below Mildred's and, more than Allegra, are the catalysts of her development. Helena is an anthropologist just back from doing field work in Africa. Another nonexcellent woman for the spinster to study at close hand, Helena is pretty, careless, and sloppy at womanly chores. She is far from reliable emotionally, since she has an unsuitable penchant for Everard Bone, a fellow anthropologist. When she mentions that her absent husband is named Rockingham, Mildred responds to the name "as if it had been a precious jewel in the dustbin." The reality matches the romance she finds in the name. Before joining his wife in London, he was flag lieutenant in Italy to an admiral whose social life he arranged. As Helena describes it, his work customarily involved being charming to dowdy Wren officers, a duty for which Rocky is admirably suited. He is one of those men whose automatic and democratic charm is not meant to be taken too personally. Inevitably, Mildred falls in love with him.

Rocky jokingly tells Mildred one day that he will educate her, and this is what he and Helena indeed do. Initially, Mildred sees herself as very competent in social situations:

> Platitudes flowed easily from me, perhaps because, with my parochial experience, I know myself to be capable of dealing with most of the stock situations or even the great moments of life—birth, marriage, death, the successful jumble sale, the garden fête spoilt by bad weather. (6)

As she becomes more and more involved with the Napiers, however, she realizes continually that they present new situations and types with which she does not know how to deal. There is the novelty of being charmed with attention and compliments, which leads to the even more unsettling experience of loving, however innocently, a married man. Mildred remarks that she is unused to dealing with handsome men; suddenly she has two of them around, Rocky and Everard Bone. They add, she thinks, a new dimension to her life, being the only two people she has ever known "who could be described as splendid and romantic." While Rocky teaches Mildred to vary the incessant tea with an occasional drink, his discontented wife teaches her to think and talk about men as more or less attractive. Unfortunately, she does not know any platitudes to smooth over serious arguments between a married couple, tensions arising from Helena's attraction to Everard, hints of Rocky's infidelities, the squabbles of separation, or the threat of divorce.

Falling in love with Rocky, Mildred falls willy-nilly into a story of her own, a drama no less important for being submerged beneath the noisier ones of the others. She first expresses her longings at her annual lunch with William Caldicote. William is a comic parallel to Rocky: just as the handsome naval officer flirted "kindly" but meaninglessly with the Wrens, so the "grey-looking" civil servant makes himself feel good by regularly throwing crumbs to the pigeons outside his office window. In an unguarded moment, after Mildred describes her new neighbors, she remarks that Rocky is "just the kind of person" she should have liked for herself. Indignantly, William declares that she must not marry, and adds:

> We, my dear Mildred, are the observers of life. Let other people get married by all means, the more the merrier. . . . Let Dora [William's sister] marry if she likes. She hasn't your talent for observation. (70)

After spending an evening with Rocky and experiencing an uncharacteristic "disturbed feeling," she decides William was right: "I must not allow myself to have feelings, but must only observe the effects of other people's."

After Rocky comes into her life, Mildred begins to smarten up her mousiness. She buys a hat because she does not want to embarrass the Napiers when she attends a meeting of Helena's Learned Society. Some time later, when Dora arrives for a visit, she remarks that her friend looks different, and Mildred admits to herself that she has taken to using more make-up, fixing her hair more carefully, and wearing slightly more colorful clothes because of the Napiers. She is annoyed, seeing her friend's underwear drying in the kitchen, at the realization that it is like her own: practical and dull. When she tries unsuccessfully to encourage Dora to buy a becoming dress, her annoyance is disproportionate— Mildred is rejecting her old self in her cheerfully dowdy friend. She startles the disapproving Dora by implying that she would not mind being one of Rocky's "Playthings": "Perhaps it's better to be unhappy than not to feel anything at all." Mildred's discussion with Rocky, following her chance meeting with a Wren who knew him in Italy, comes too late to help her. He admits that he hardly remembers any of the many women who fell in love with him and complains that women

> take their pleasures very sadly. Few of them know how to run light-hearted flirtations—the nice ones, that is. They cling on to those little bits of romance that may have happened years ago. *Semper Fidelis*, you know. (137)

Especially when Mildred remarks that this was her old school motto, one alternative for her future is clear: here we have a potential Belinda Bede.

Mildred suffers when Rocky leaves for his cottage in the country, but her feelings begin to fade, diluted by the absence of his charm and his failure to follow up on a careless invitation for a day together. Eventually, he returns to announce his reconciliation with Helena (a rapprochement initiated by the letter Helena asked their go-between to write) and their decision to live in the country. By now, Mildred feels as strong as the tea she brews at Rocky's request. Under the guise of discussing Helena and Everard Bone and a hypothetical instance of disillusion, she discusses her relationship with Rocky. As she sees it now, his mild romancing was meaningless: "he only did it because he felt it was expected of him." Rocky suggests that such a man may have been "kind to you when you needed kindness—surely that's worth something?" Mildred cannot disagree:

> Once more, perhaps for the last time, I saw the Wren officers huddled together in an awkward little group on the terrace of the Admiral's villa. Rocky's kindness must surely have meant a great deal to them at that moment and perhaps some of them would never forget it as long as they lived. (225)

Rocky's description of his flirtations as "kindness" is self-serving, though Mildred accepts it. Still, serious bitterness is out of the question not only because the character of our civilian Wren precludes it, but also because she has gained so much from her entanglement with the messy Napiers.

Helena's fruitless pursuit of Everard discloses that even a nonexcellent woman may conceive an "irrational passion" for an unsuitable object and be "the rejected one"; unlike her less-demanding counterpart, though, she goes after what she wants. The desirability of taking positive action on one's own behalf is underlined when Rocky responds to Mildred's veiled reproach for his failure to extend a specific invitation: "But people mustn't wait to be asked. Other people came." In the same conversation, Rocky, like William Caldicote, causes her to face the question of observation versus participation, of whether she is content "contriving" others' affairs. Mildred is forced to reflect: "perhaps I did love it as I always seemed to get involved in them, I thought with resignation; perhaps I really enjoyed other people's lives more than my own." But this is the thought of a disheartened moment. Unwittingly, Rocky has already given Mildred the gift of her own feelings, her own story. From her initial resolution to observe but not experience emotion, to her declaration of the superiority of unhappiness to emotional nothingness, Mildred's outlook has changed. It is true that the loving-and-losing plot she enacted in the privacy of her heart finally displeases and fails to "ennoble" her, whatever that means. But the seductive Rocky forced Mildred to recognize the feelings, needs, and aspirations that she formerly tried to disown and suppress.

Helena Napier enlarges Mildred's world by introducing her to another community as small and well-defined as that of St. Mary's, the Learned Society of anthropologists. In addition to Helena, Everard Bone and Esther Clovis are its chief representatives in the novel. Mildred dislikes the "romantic and splendid" Everard from the beginning, and has to "make it a Lent resolution to try to like him." Opportunities to practice virtue on him present themselves, and almost imperceptibly her feelings begin to change. At first, Everard seeks her out because he wants help in warding off Helena's unwelcome advances. Later, after the threat posed by the aggressive woman is over, he continues his invitations. But Mildred, involved in the kind of unsuitable attachment so perfectly suited to an excellent woman (since it is not reciprocal and cannot threaten her spinsterhood), incapable of believing that a splendid man might be interested in her, does not perceive his attention as personal and is sometimes annoyed when he turns up. Used to her role as go-between, she assumes he wants information about the troublesome Helena. But she often finds herself thinking of Everard after Rocky leaves, though she admits, characteristically, to no particular feelings for him. Attracted to Everard, she is so used to repressing her feelings that she has no vocabulary for expressing them. However, the woman who denied any similarity to Jane Eyre imagines Bone, when she has not seen him for awhile, lying sick and alone "with nobody to look after him."

Pym gives the novel a sly twist with Esther Clovis, employee of the Learned Society. Everard invites Mildred to lunch and, apropos of Helena's inconvenient attraction for him, remarks that he intends to marry eventually, if he can find a suitable, sensible woman:

> "Somebody who would help you in your work?" I suggested. "Somebody with a knowledge of anthropology who could correct proofs and make an index, rather like Miss Clovis, perhaps?"
> "Esther Clovis is certainly a very capable person," he said doubtfully. "An excellent woman altogether."
> "You could consider marrying an excellent woman?" I asked in amazement. "But they are not for marrying."
> "You're surely not suggesting that they are for the other things?" he said, smiling. (189)

There have been signs that Miss Clovis might be of Mildred's species: just as Mildred took in Winifred Malory when she quarreled with Allegra, Esther took in Helena (and collected her clothes) when she left Rocky. The irony is delightful. Mildred finds a man who might consider marrying an excellent woman, but learns that, in Everard's particular community, Miss Clovis holds the title: she has the qualifications (as Mildred has not) to give the particular kind of assistance most required by the male anthropologist. Mildred is flabbergasted. Altogether, Everard's ideas about marriage are more practical than romantic, as even she realizes when he discusses deliberately looking for a suitable wife. When he goes on to say that he respects and esteems Miss Clovis, she disparages such sentiments as "dry bones" and shows uncharacteristic cattiness: "Miss Clovis must be quite a lot older than you are, and then she looks so odd. She has hair like a dog." Of course, she feels guilty immediately, but also decides to send Everard a postcard when she goes on vacation. Splendid men who would marry an excellent woman do not, after all, grow on trees.

Everard responds to the brazen postcard with an invitation to dinner at his apartment. His timing could not be worse. Mildred has just had to cope with Julian and Winifred's troubles over his broken engagement and is "exhausted with bearing other people's burdens." She is "feeling tired," her face "quite grey," her reward for being the selfless "woman with no troubles of her own, who takes a kindly interest in those of her friends." She does not even want to answer the telephone when Everard calls, "wondering whose voice would come out of it and what it would ask [her] to do." Being the go-between and helper, Mildred has learned, involves more than having a privileged snooping position: she is carrying the others' emotional burdens. When Everard announces that he has "some meat to cook," she has the horrible vision of bending, with her aching back, over a sink to prepare vegetables. She declines his invitation. But as she mulls it over, her guilt (for refusing to fix his dinner) gives way to the recognition of other feelings: it matters very much to her to know that she was his "first choice."

As soon as Rocky and Helena have left permanently, Mildred ambles into action to pursue a relationship with Everard. (Significantly, in their last conversation, the Napiers call Mildred "a good woman," as if they recognize that she has changed.) Discarding the zany idea of joining the Prehistoric Society of which Everard is a member, she decides to wait to see him at Lent services. But, finally, she cannot wait until "Lenten is come with love to town." As she walks calculatedly by the premises of the Learned Society, she wonders, "Is there no end to the humiliations we subject ourselves to?" Her strategic stroll pays off in an impromptu lunch with Everard and another dinner invitation. Unasked, she promises to cook the meat and immediately feels better, though she recognizes that it is "a burden in a way and yet perhaps because of being a burden, a pleasure." Though she goes prepared to cook, she also goes prepared to take on Esther Clovis, whom she assumes will be there. Anticipating an all-out battle, Mildred dresses herself to "look like the kind of person who could not possibly" proofread or make an index. Since Miss Clovis has seemingly cornered the role of excellent woman, Mildred believes her best plan is to appear as the nonexcellent woman—the one who usually gets her man—and models her dress on Helena's. She does not believe she has succeeded, but her appearance makes a friend and William Caldicote take notice: usually "one scarcely remembers" how she looks; this evening she looks "*triste*."

As it turns out, Everard has not invited Miss Clovis to dinner, and Mildred does not have to cook. He has other tasks in mind for her. His design is to tailor Mildred into the male anthropologist's version of the good woman: he will teach her how to read proof on his book, and for variety, he suggests, she can also learn how to do its index. Mildred protests in vain. When she agrees, at last, she knows precisely what she is doing:

> Was any man worth this burden? Probably not, but one shouldered it bravely and cheerfully and in the end it might turn out to be not so heavy after all. (255)

Mildred's use of "burden" points to her realization that emotional involvement may cost her autonomy and tranquillity. Her reluctance to do Everard's scholarly chores, like her earlier refusal to cook his meal, is also her tiny effort to heed Mrs. Morris's lesson about Julian (which applies also to Rocky): she does not want to serve Everard's needs and then get left in the end. But this is different, a case in which self-sacrifice is indistinguishable from self-interest. Her optimistic willingness to serve Everard has a lot to do with his earlier remark that proofreading and making indexes is "what wives are for," a remark he follows up with a reference to the wife of the late president of the Learned Society (a wife who did not understand anthropology any more than Mildred does).

Her disclaimers notwithstanding, Mildred has a story, after all. The all-important question of whether she is to be observer or participant in life was decided when she fell in love with Rocky, a decision confirmed by her attraction to, and sedate pursuit of, Everard. We must conclude that if Mildred has not heretofore been given to falling in love, such emotional sloth was due to the dearth of good-looking men at St. Mary's. Her feeling for the anthropologist, we assume, "must be a different kind of love, neither weaker nor stronger than the first [affection for Rocky], perhaps not to be compared at all." But her story is not simply about an unsuitable love and disillusion followed by a suitable attraction and its promise for the future.

As the preceding remarks indicate, Mildred's real story details her corruption, her ruination as a pure model of an excellent woman. Not only her looks have changed by the time she goes off hoping to make poor Miss Clovis look bad, hoping to enchant Everard. At a church-bazaar meeting, she has risked her reputation as a sane woman by inquiring whether tea is really needed, by suggesting that Julian absent himself though "the vicar has always presided," by asking needless questions, and by snapping at the mealy-mouthed Miss Enders, who criticizes Helena. At the end of the evening she feels has been wasted, she remarks that after what has happened, "Nothing can ever be really the same . . . even if it appears to be from the outside." With Rocky's departure, Mildred started getting tired of others' problems, a fatigue brought to its lowest point when she had to console Winifred and Julian in quick succession. As soon as Mildred grows tired of burdens which yield her nothing but weariness, a gray face, and dirty teacups, her days as a selfless helper, confidante, or go-between are over. She might as well expend on her own affairs the effort and energy she expends on others' business. Proof that Mildred is no longer an excellent woman is supplied by Julian and Everard, who see her as a potential wife. The undiscerning Julian may think she is still excellent, but with the "Hawaiian Fire" and the rest, the Mildred he looks at with interest is not the woman he earlier imagined he wounded and rejected.

Though Everard thinks her sensible, he never really thought of her as an excellent woman. Mildred was often huffy and irritable with him, and refused to cook that meal for him. Besides, in his circle, Esther Clovis is the excellent woman whom one may respect and admire without inviting to dinner.

Mildred's selflessness and passivity, the prime characteristics of the excellent woman, are gone. The burden of Everard, especially, has the virtue of being one she chooses to carry (even before she agrees to read proof) for a man she finds attractive. It is no accident that she looks happily toward a future of doing her "duty" by two men after each has hinted he might do his duty toward her—by marrying her:

> So, what with my duty there ["protecting" Julian] and the work I was going to do for Everard, it seemed as if I might be going to have what Helena called "a full life" after all. (256)

The old-fashioned Mildred can express her anticipated involvement with the men only as "duty," in the context of submission to her religious or moral obligation to help others. As she did earlier in the novel, she defines her purpose from the needs of others; the difference is that, responding to the needs of Julian and Everard, Mildred responds to her own particular emotional needs and makes the effort to satisfy them. Thinking about "duty," she sounds as resigned as a cat who has been asked to guard a couple of canaries. At the end of the novel, on an imaginary pole with "excellent woman" at one extreme and "sly vixen" on the other, she is a good woman somewhere in the middle range, leaning ever so slightly toward the latter extreme.

Though she can have few illusions about marriage after watching Helena and Rocky, Mildred belongs to a class and generation of women for whom marriage is the greatest good. Her reflections when she and Dora go to an Old Girls' Reunion indicate that she is realistic. In this milieu, she knows that more than any accomplishment or distinction, "It was the ring on the left hand that people . . . looked for." Representing, as she thinks, a "full life," the ring matters to her, too. She realizes that her classmates' husbands are probably more "uninteresting" than she and Dora imagine, but, on the other hand, she thinks some might be "distinguished and handsome." There is no doubt that Mildred wants to marry, but she does not wish to marry just anyone. Though she is too practical to close off the option, she does not fall into Julian's arms when the scales fall from his eyes. She "respects and esteems" him, and coyly thinks it might be her "duty" to marry him. But she pursues Everard, whom she considers "splendid" and handsome. However Everard might or might not feel about her, she is attracted to and ready to fall in love with him. As far as Pym is concerned, Mildred's happy ending is her decision to honor herself by making her best effort to fulfill her own desires and emotional needs.

Jane and Prudence

Jane and Prudence deals with Jane and Nicholas Cleveland as they settle into a country parish, with the friendship of Jane and Prudence Bates, and with Jane's effort to marry Prudence to a suitable man. Prudence lives in London, but the women see each other fairly frequently, and the novel moves occasionally from the village where Nicholas Cleveland is vicar of the parish church to London, especially to Prudence's office. Though the superficial differences between the women are obvious, Pym gives them significant similarities: each has a remarkably active imagination, and each is greatly affected by a literary model she has more or less selected for herself. In addition to being an influence on the individual's vision of herself, the feminine imagination, activated by love or the mere gender difference, works on men, recreating them in certain ways. *Jane and Prudence*, then, treats the effect of the imagination on the relations between the sexes, the way women see themselves and their lives, and the way they see men. In addition to the power of the imagination, the novel's other themes include the needs of "Man," the feminine subservience to those needs, the issue of unfulfilled promise, and the question of what men want.

It is clear early in the novel that each woman has adopted a literary role as a model for herself. Officially, the world of Jane and Prudence has a limited number of acceptable categories for women. Eleanor Hitchins, Prudence's college friend and a single career woman, assumes that "one had to settle down sooner or later into the comfortable spinster or the contented or bored wife." Eleanor herself is very happy with her life as a spinster, a single career woman. Prudence, however, has chosen another option for herself. She has adopted the part of the romantic heroine, while Jane is saddled with the model of the helpmate. Both are roles adopted for the sake of love and are models of women in relation to men. The helpmate exists, as her name indicates, to aid a man in his endeavors, to reduce herself, for love, to a pair of willing hands for the use of the more important male. She finds her true fulfillment in serving his needs and goals. The romantic heroine, while not officially or irrevocably committed to a man, cannot be reduced to hands. She is still those eyes, those lips, and if she is hands at all, they are soft, white hands—upon which no sensible male would impose a burden. Though the heroine and the helpmate seem to be opposites, and though their stories are usually told separately, they are phases of the same fictional woman; marriage, it was traditionally assumed, transforms the heroine into the helpmate. Obviously, the romantic heroine exists to be admired, to be loved, and, finally, to be married.

But the heroine of the interchangeable romantic novel Prudence is always reading is a variation on the type, figuring in a plot with an "inevitable but satisfying unhappy ending." We can easily outline this novel. Its heroine is refined and beautiful, her lover handsome, passionate, and incredibly romantic. Though (or because) their love is crossed in some way, it is very profound—but, finally, it cannot be. They part so the heroine can suffer deeply (without any loss of beauty), so she can assume an attractive tragic posture. She ends as she began, alone in the spotlight at center stage. The sentimental appeal of the plot is tremendous, since it has it both ways, balancing fulfillment with loss, great joy with great sorrow. The beautiful Prudence, who has the habit of imagining herself as she thinks others see her, has the basic heroine material. Indeed, remembering one of her homelier admirers, she declares without embarrassment that they were like Beauty and the Beast. As for refinement, she reads the poetry of Coventry Patmore in public and drops literary quotations into her conversation and letters.

Prudence's life is superficially pleasant, thanks in large part to the care she lavishes on herself. She dresses well, has an elegant apartment, treats herself as a matter of course to good food and drink, and is generally kind to herself. Her sole concern, triggered by the startled looks of a very young man, is whether there is a "falling off" in her beauty and ability to attract men. The only thing missing in her life is some kind of abiding emotional focus or interest outside of herself. Her job at a "vague cultural organisation" for Arthur Grampian, a historian or economist whose books no one reads, is mechanical and so uninteresting she cannot describe it. At the Reunion of Old Students at Oxford that opens the novel, her former tutor refers to those women who have their families and those who have their careers. But she falters when she comes to Prudence, and Jane thinks, "She might have said, 'and Prudence has her love affairs' . . . for they were surely as much an occupation as anything else." Prudence's series of love affairs is her career. Her passion and commitment, however, do not seem to be given to any of the men she "loves" in turn.

Jane Cleveland fell into the literary model that she can neither emulate nor reject. When she fell in love with Nicholas at Oxford, she had no idea he was to be a clergyman. However, once engaged, she started

> imagining herself as a clergyman's wife, starting with Trollope and working through the Victorian novelists to the present-day gallant, cheerful wives, who ran large houses and families on far too little money and sometimes wrote articles about it in the *Church Times*. (8)

Here, too, we know the plot. The capable and endlessly resourceful woman married to a country vicar is the self-effacing pillar of strength to whom the entire community looks for cheerful help and quiet guidance. She is especially helpful to her husband in dealing with the human problems presented by his flock, smoothing hurt feelings, resolving parishioners' quarrels. She has her great moment when, her husband unjustly vilified, accused, or somehow threatened, she stands by her man with the loyalty and courage that keeps him going until he is vindicated. All of this is in addition, of course, to raising a large brood and running a model household on pitifully slender means.

Unfortunately, considering the model stuck in her mind, Jane does not have the personality or the interest in domestic competence to be the vicar's superwife. Though pretty, she cannot be bothered to adjust a showing slip, and this carelessness extends to the other aspects of her life. She has a hectic manner, speaks too enthusiastically and loudly, and speaks often and thoughtlessly, following her own quirky line of thought while happily oblivious of her audience. She has a genuine gift for the inapposite quotation, the most striking example involving Bishop King's "Exequy." The lines beginning "Stay for me there, I will not fail / To meet thee in that hollow vale" rise to her lips apropos of a widower on the verge of remarriage. Nicholas often tries to cut off her fanciful or inappropriate verbal flights and tends to walk away from her as she chatters on.

As the vicar's wife, Jane is barely interested in matters concerning the church and has no idea how to extend the minimal hospitalities to visitors at the vicarage. Unlike her model, she was unable to have more than one child, and even the eighteen-year-old Flora, before she goes off to Oxford for her first year, demonstrates a greater skill at "womanly" tasks than her mother possesses. Jane is a disaster as a housekeeper. Since she cannot cook and feels incompetent even to pour tea, Mrs. Glaze, their housekeeper, takes care of all the practical details while Jane looks for any excuse "to absent herself from parish duties." She seems to spend a lot of time wandering around doing nothing. Jane makes no effort whatever to overcome her domestic disabilities; in fact, unless she is feeling guilty, she ignores her incapacity to do what is assumed to be women's work.

Like Prudence, Jane exists primarily in the world of the imagination, but unlike her friend, she is largely an observer of others. She imagines a history for practically anyone who catches her attention and, given the chance, elaborates on it. Despite her absentminded friendliness, she is mostly self-involved: people and their affairs interest her mainly because they satisfy her curiosity or fire her "vivid fancy." The individuals and situations she hears of when she first comes to the village inspire her to say, "We are like people coming into the cinema in the middle of a film . . . at the best we have a bald and garbled synopsis whispered to us by somebody on his way out."

The women's models involve the issue of failed promise, in the particular spheres of career and relationships. Jane, thinking especially of the scholarly work she abandoned when she married, remarks at the Oxford reunion that none of the women present has really fulfilled her early potential. Pym never reveals why, with only one child and minimal involvement in her household and her husband's parish, Jane put aside her work after publishing a book of essays. We are left to conclude that she assumed, as everyone does in the novel, that women "have" either their families or their careers. She willingly exchanged a self-chosen role in which she was competent for the ready-made role dictated by Nicholas's work, a role she can play only badly.

Jane failed to fulfill the promise of her own interests and has been unable or unwilling to replace them with the interests of her chosen literary model. One is tempted to conclude that subconsciously she is paying back Nicholas for having robbed her of her own primacy to herself, but it hardly matters since her disappointment turns inward. Abandoning her interests and ignoring those she believes she should pursue, Jane has a conviction of personal uselessness and lives a strangely unfocused existence.

Though she is not privy to her friend's dissatisfactions, Prudence feels that compared with Jane's life, hers is "rich and full of promise" because she can fall in love as often as she wishes. Prudence's "promise" is the anticipation that better and more excellent loves than she has previously known await her in the future. At any time, she thinks, she can take her choice from the "lines of eligible and delightful men" she imagines. But since she does not think in terms of one love, of one eligible and delightful man, the promise she treasures is really a promise of many sad or unhappy endings.

The model each woman has assumed dictates self-defeating behavior. Prudence goes out of her way to insure frustration in love. In her office, there are several women, but only two men, Arthur Grampian and Geoffrey Manifold. Grampian is married and forty-eight, Manifold single and thirty— so naturally Prudence has chosen Grampian. Jane, despite the awareness of her long record of failure in the role, does not discard the helpmate model. Instead, she imagines pathos in Mr. Oliver, one of her husband's quarrelsome parishioners, and invites him to tea: Nicholas tells her the invitation may fuel the rivalries in which Oliver figures. Walking by the church one day, she hears men arguing in the choir vestry and imagines "herself mediating and bringing them together so that they all went off and settled their differences over a glass of beer": they consider her "importunate" and tell her it is none of her business. Because the parish church council has been combative, she encourages Nicholas to make its meeting sociable by having it in the vicarage, and then speaks thoughtlessly about a sensitive issue: "not for the first time," Nicholas thinks there is "something to be said for the celibacy of the clergy." Inspired by their literary models, both women act in ways that must cause them sadness, frustration, or a loss of self-esteem.

Just as Prudence and Jane have imagined selves, they and most of the women in the novel collaborate in imagining "Man," creating a mysterious being with unique problems and pressing needs that women must alleviate. Jane and Jessie Morrow have an occasional satirical thought, but at various points, we learn that Man needs breakfast; Man needs eggs; Man needs the scarce meat of postwar rations; Man needs company more than self-sufficient women do; Man needs to have his fatigue publicly recognized; and most especially, Man needs a lot of love to ease the exclusively male burdens that he carries: "Men did not have quite the same trials as women—it would be the larger things that worried him, his health, his work." On one occasion, when the proprietor of the village cafe serves a young man roast chicken that is not on the menu, Jane is present: "Man needs bird, she thought. Just the very best, that is what man needs."

In spite of her rebellious thought, Jane's own continual feeling of inadequacy springs from her failure to meet what she considers her husband's special needs. She acted in the past and continues to act as if Nicholas, by mere virtue of being a man and her husband, requires the sacrifice of her interests and talents to his success and well-being. Moreover, she and Prudence find a special pathos in men everywhere they look. Jane imagines the drab and lonely bachelor lives of Mr. Oliver and Fabian Driver. Apparently, Mrs. Crampton, the proprietor of the cafe, and Mrs. Walton, a landlady, preceded Jane in sighing over Mr. Oliver's hard case, and one provides him with special dishes, the other with a "very nice front room" complete with ornamental fern. Fabian, far from fending ineptly for himself, as Jane supposes, has a very competent housekeeper. Prudence practically sheds tears over a stranger in a cafeteria whose overheard conversation reveals that his wife is in the hospital. On another occasion, on her way to visit Jane by train, she sees a man carrying a cakebox and is teary-eyed and almost overcome by her sentimental assumption that he is "a good husband and father." It is as if any hint of a difficulty found men uniquely weak and vulnerable; as if any hint of male thoughtfulness were as marvelous as an unexpected thank-you note from the family cat. In the novel, the women collaborate to create the masculine helplessness and needs that keep them in subjugation.

The re-creation of men by women is especially noticeable in love. At the beginning of the novel, Jane has heard of Arthur Grampian but never seen him. What she imagines is "a big, tall, dark man, a sort of Mr. Rochester"; what she sees when she meets him is an "insignificant-looking little man." She remarks to herself on this occasion, and again later, that women are doing a "splendid" thing for men all the time:

> that was why women were so wonderful; it was their love and imagination that transformed these unremarkable beings. For most men, when one came to think of it, were undistinguished to look at, if not positively ugly. (217)

Although we may object that men as often as women labor like ancient idolaters to create an image worthy of their worship, Jane's insight holds true in the novel. In regard to Grampian, Jane and Prudence can only agree that they see him differently; however, one beautiful man does not need to be loved into splendor. Fabian Driver is the particular focus of the feminine imagination in Jane's village. His late wife Constance, who "brought him a comfortable amount of money as well as a great deal of love," entertained Fabian's women friends from time to time and spent the rest of her time doing needlework. Fabian thinks it is time, after a year, to stop playing the "inconsolable widower." He is ready to resume his career as a lover.

Since he is generally known to have been unfaithful to the worthy Constance, Fabian inspires a naughty fascination in the females of the neighborhood, who frequently compare him to a lion. The first time Jane sees him, he bestows a large marrow on the women decorating the church for the Harvest Thanksgiving:

> "What a fine marrow, Mr. Driver," said Miss Doggett in a bright tone. "It is the biggest one we have had so far, isn't it, Miss Morrow?"
>
> Miss Morrow, who was scrabbling on the floor among the vegetables, mumbled something inaudible.
>
> "It is magnificent," said Mrs. Mayhew reverently.
>
> Mr. Driver moved forward and presented the marrow to Miss Doggett with something of a flourish.
>
> Jane felt as if she were assisting at some primitive kind of ritual at whose significance she hardly dared to guess. (31)

Given his past and his marrow, it is not surprising that Fabian makes the respectable Miss Doggett remember that "They say . . . men only want *one thing*." Even Jane sees him as a romantic figure and is seriously disappointed to observe that he dresses for the weather and carries an umbrella on a country walk. It does not occur to her that he is not responsible for, or obliged to live up to, the demands of her imagination—she is as outraged as if she had discovered Lord Byron filling his hot-water bottle. For failing to live up to her image of him, Fabian is treated to Jane's uncharacteristic hostility, and he "maliciously" retaliates by noticing all the flaws in her appearance.

Despite Fabian's little faults, Jane decides she will play the role of Pandarus or Jane Austen's Emma Woodhouse. (Typically, she forgets the outcome of Pandarus's efforts and of Emma's ambitions for Harriet Smith.) Providing Prudence with a suitable prospect, Jane makes a mistake and sets in motion the novel's main conflicts. The first is between what she wants for Prudence and what Prudence wants for herself. Though Jane knows her friend has "got into the way of preferring unsatisfactory love affairs to any others, so that it was becoming almost a bad habit," she assumes the glamorous Prudence wants, or should want, to marry. It does not occur to her that her own hazy aura of uselessness and dissatisfaction might make an observer question the necessity or value of marriage. Nicholas, as I mentioned before, has occasional misgivings, and Jane herself thinks several times that "mild, kindly looks and spectacles" are the eventual, inevitable conclusion of love and passion. Obviously, her marriage has not lived up to her imagination. She and Nicholas are fond of each other, but in a dull, placid sort of way. From Prudence's point of view, Jane's marriage looks even less like an advertisement for something desirable. She intercepts an exasperated look between the Clevelands and observes that they create a "peculiar kind of desolation" wherever they live. She believes her friend's intellectual gifts are wasted in parish life and senses Jane's unfocused discontentment.

Traditionally, successful love leads the heroine to the ever-after of wedded bliss, but Prudence wishes to linger endlessly in the romantic antechamber. She cherishes her mental list of ex-lovers, a gallery reminiscent of Andrew Marvell's, except that hers is populated by several men. However, she is not big on self-analysis or knowledge, and she recognizes Fabian's suitability as a possible husband. His good looks, combined with hers, would make them a gorgeous couple, and they are a challenge to her. And so, with her half-hearted participation, she and Fabian begin a superficial but romantically impeccable affair. Here is another version of Beauty and the Beast for Prudence, with the difference that the lion has a beauty of his own. But the problem with the suitable Fabian is that he cannot live up to the standard of her imagination. Having a charming little dinner with him one evening, a mental comparison of her imaginary evenings with Grampian leaves her disappointed in Fabian's banality. However, what his company or conversation fail to accomplish is achieved by wine and good food: Prudence is exhilarated by the meal to the extent that she thinks "perhaps she really did admire Fabian." In truth, Fabian is as lukewarm as she, and tacky to boot. More than by Prudence's seeming interest, he is gratified by proof (as he thinks) that he has "not lost his old touch." Eventually, he presents her with a poetry book inscribed with a quotation from Marvell's "The Definition of Love"—a copy of the same book with the same inscription given him by his late wife. Ironically, neither the nominal lovers nor Jane realizes that the poem describes an utterly impossible passion, parallel loves that "can never meet"—hardly what the matchmaker had in mind.

Jane, when the relationship is slow to advance to an offer of marriage, urges Prudence, who seems confident that the offer will be made, to propose to Fabian herself. Prudence is not interested in bringing matters to a crisis, which is understandable, since there is no indication, at any stage of her relationship with Fabian, that she has any special feelings about him. Though she enjoys being courted and even seems to be willing to marry him, she remains detached and palpably cool about him. She probably senses, too, that he is as unattached emotionally as she is. Fabian is as used to admiration as Prudence; consequently neither gets enough from the other to feel sufficiently gratified. Besides, Prudence intimidates the mighty lion. Her friendship with the vicar's wife inhibits him, making him feel that theirs cannot be a sexual relationship. Moreover, he fears that she expects more romantically than he can comfortably provide. Even her letters, full of literary quotations, are hard for him to answer. It is very difficult for him to remember the bon mots of Oscar Wilde. Truly, these parallel loves can never meet: the relationship stalls on their equal self-involvement.

The external conflict, unknown to all but two of the characters, is between Prudence and Jessie Morrow for the post of lion-keeper. Although Miss Doggett is basically unchanged from her earlier incarnation in *Crampton Hodnet*, Jessie seems altogether less drab, though she is not nearly as attractive as Prudence: she is thirty-seven, dresses badly (according to Fabian), and has a "birdlike little face with long nose and large bright eyes." She has no discernible imagination with regard to Fabian, feeling no need to recreate him from the raw material she knows very well.

Jessie does not have much imagination about herself, either. Unlike Prudence (or Jane), she attempts to make herself into no model, and admits she cannot hope to compete on the basis of looks. Once only, while she lays her plans and examines herself in the mirror, does she feel "like a character in a novel." Unlike Prudence, she has no interest in hankering indefinitely after an impossible someone; she takes charge by secretly pursuing Fabian when she can get away from Miss Doggett. Evidently, Jessie's active interest, undisguised admiration, and undemanding approach captivate Fabian, though there is the implication that she has also given him the *one thing*, the only thing that men want. Imagination figures in this relationship much less prominently than in Prudence's. But here, significantly, it is Fabian who thinks, after Jessie has sparked his interest, that "it would be interesting to see her transformed in the way that the women's magazines sometimes glamorized a dowdy woman." The masculine imagination is evidently not as powerful as the feminine, which can actually effect the transformation, but it does exist.

Jessie's projected marriage to Fabian should be very romantic as the heartwarming triumph of the plain heroine over a more glamorous rival. But Pym explodes the idea that marriage is the true fulfillment awaiting the romantic heroine through Jane's marriage and her reflections. In retrospect, when she ponders her friend's lukewarm feelings for Fabian, she remembers that "at times [Prudence] found him boring and irritating. But wasn't that what so many marriages were—finding a person boring and irritating and yet loving him? Who could imagine a man who was *never* boring or irritating?" We see what Jane means, of course, but boredom and irritation are not recognized aspects of romantic love and perhaps the tolerance or even the taste for them can be acquired only slowly, through the years. Certainly, it is too much to expect Prudence, fed by romantic novels and by her own fertile imagination, to settle for a man who bores and irritates her from the start.

Jane and Prudence seems to be a novel about failure: Nicholas fails to resolve a minor rift among some parishioners, Jane fails at matchmaking, and Prudence fails at capturing Fabian, if we can call it failure not to achieve something she did not really desire. In fact, given her literary model, Prudence succeeds, getting an unsatisfactory affair from which she can extract a delicious sadness. There is also a payoff for Jane when Miss Doggett decides that the vicar's wife is the proper person to consult about Jessie and Fabian. At last, the helpmate springs into action, confronting the culprits and persuading Fabian to break the news to Prudence. Jane's heart aches for the rejected one, but Pym is at her best describing Prudence eating a "solitary" meal at a chic restaurant on the day she hears the news.

Prudence's "suffering" goes no deeper than her "love." Since she makes impossible choices (as she does with Grampian), or makes her choices impossible (as she does with Fabian), for her being in love and suffering are two stages of the same thing. The truest aspect of her sadness is the feeling that her life is "blank." It is, but not because of losing Fabian, in himself: Prudence's life is empty without a man, any man she can "love"— and use in her enactment of the romantic heroine. Her frightening blankness lasts for less than two days, when she is blessed with a new interest in Geoffrey Manifold. After he consoles her, she is happy enough to relegate Fabian to her gallery of ex-lovers: "Philip, Henry, Laurence, Peter, Fabian and who could tell how many others there might be?" The newly vacant room in her heart of hearts is filled by Geoffrey, whom she has been busily recreating into an interesting, pathetic object. Once again, the visiting Jane wonders at the power of women to transform "an ordinary and colourless" man into an object of interest. Prudence tells her that "everything would be spoilt if anything came of" the relationship and adds, with a smile, "We shall probably hurt each other very much before it's finished, but we're doomed really." This is bliss, obviously. Jane realizes that there is no reason why Geoffrey Manifold should be an impossible, tragic love, and there is none—except for Prudence's determination to convince herself that she feels by "suffering."

The novel ends where its main action started, with the same situation. Jane, under the pretext of buying the same confirmation books she failed to get the first time, comes to lunch with her friend in the city. They eat at the same restaurant, where they see the same people, and Jane meets Prudence's love, who inspires the same thought about feminine love's transforming power. Prudence, who does not perceive the repetition, will retrace the same pattern. But Jane suddenly realizes that "one's life followed a kind of pattern, with the same things cropping up again and again"—and determines to be a better helpmate. To rededicate herself and conform to her literary model, she actually buys the confirmation books. However, when she meets Edward Lyall, the village's member of Parliament, her idea of making a match between him and Prudence so enthralls her that she almost walks off without her parcel of books. Clearly, her past failures have taught her nothing that enables her to change. In the end, then, despite Jane's insight, both women are still under the grip of imaginative models that lead them only to discontentment and unfulfillment.

Together with other things, Jessie's success and Prudence's failure hint at some answers to the question raised by the novel: what do men want? It is obviously not glamour, and it is not only the *one thing*, although this factor may play into it. Nicholas's conclusion (though drawn intermittently and without much hostility) that Jane is unsatisfactory as a wife suggests that some men want a woman capable of serving their career and domestic needs. Some want, in other words, what Jane aspires to be, a helpmate devoted to their well-being. This view is discussed when Miss Doggett describes the relationship of a newly married couple she has heard of, Mildred Lathbury and Everard Bone:

> "He is a brilliant man," said Miss Doggett. "She helped him a good deal in his work, I think. Mrs. Bonner says that she even learned to type so that she could type his manuscripts for him."
>
> "Oh, then he had to marry her," said Miss Morrow sharply. "That kind of devotion is worse than blackmail—a man has no escape from that."
>
> "No, one does feel that," Jane agreed. "Besides, he would be quite sure that she would be a useful wife," she added a little sadly, thinking of her own failures. (126)

Perhaps Jessie should not be so unkind. Though Fabian has no recognizable occupation, one can easily imagine her taking a passionate interest in sides of beef if he had been a butcher. Still, her own case suggests that, without the tangible need for a helpmate, some men want other things. What Fabian fails to get from Prudence and gets from Jessie (at least initially) is evident, plentiful admiration and a tolerant, undemanding acceptance. In short, according to the novel, men want admiring, unthreatening women who will devote themselves to promoting the men's careers and comfort without interfering or trying to change them and their foibles—women who will let them play in peace with their soap animals, as Jane puts it.

Ironically, Fabian does not realize, until he is engaged to Jessie, that she is "too sharp" to permit him, as Constance did, romantic affairs to relieve the ardors of marriage. The lion feels "as if a net had closed round him." The last time we see him, he is startled by a broken piece of statuary, the headless body of a dwarf, and made uncomfortable when Jane lifts up its bearded head. The images of diminishment and powerlessness are underscored by Jane's comment that he, escorting Jessie and Miss Doggett, is "led away captive by the women." Flora's comparison of him with Milton's blind Samson might imply hidden strength in reserve, but we remember that the hero's glorious exercise of his power meant his death. Fabian's muffled misgivings about his new situation suggest something else men might want: that, in addition to his needing love, company, and meat, women would not imagine that every Man needs Wife.

*   *   *

Jane and Prudence, with its emphasis on what women do for men and on the perceived differences between the sexes, is a good point of departure for an analysis of the love-related differences separating the sexes in Pym's early novels. The need to love, as an urgent factor motivating behavior, belongs exclusively to women. In characters like Belinda, Harriet, Mildred, and especially Prudence, we see that romantic love matters to women at any age, and that they have very high expectations of the relationship between the sexes. Men like Parnell, Mold, and the bishop, on the other hand, consider love irrelevant or inappropriate to their age; others, like Henry, Rocky, Fabian, and Arthur Grampian, desire not love but admiration, an experience of their power to attract women. Beyond the admiration of women, all expect the gratification of their desires—for a suitable wife, an auditor, a cup of tea, a dinner companion, or whatever else they happen to want.

By being primary, women's need to love, if deprived of a conventional object, causes them to experience their lives as "blankness," like Prudence, or to see themselves unhappily as "observers," like Mildred. However, it leads them also to value diverse options allowing them some degree of emotional fulfillment. Love for a sister is the foundation of Harriet and Belinda's contentment; affection for a brother defines Winifred Malory's life. An unsuitable attachment, whether it seems "unsuitable" to Pym's people by virtue of being unattainable, unethical, or incongruous, is nevertheless an option esteemed by the women. Prudence knows Arthur Grampian pays her no particular attention; Belinda and Mildred both believe it is wrong to love married men; and Harriet knows Mr. Donne is far too young for her. Still, as the archdeacon says, there it is. Men like Mold, Parnell, and William Caldicote seem content alone and deny the importance of emotion altogether (though William does seem attached to the pigeons he feeds). Neither these men nor the others expend themselves on unsuitable attachments or unattainable objects. When Belinda refuses him, Theo proposes to Connie Aspinall. Henry's fondness for Belinda does not mean shaping his daily life around her, and Edgar Donne, Rocky, and Everard Bone cherish no romantic feelings about Harriet, Mildred, or Helena, respectively. Rocky seems to speak for the majority of Pym's men when he remarks that men differ from women in not taking too seriously "little bits of romance."

Exercising the imagination is essential to Pym's women. For some, like Belinda and Prudence, imaginary pleasures not only fill the emotional gaps in actuality, but also seem superior to real events. Prudence, especially, shows how women transform ordinary men they love or want to love into interesting or lovable creatures, but Jane does the same thing for Fabian. Men may imagine a woman like Mildred into usefulness or, more fleetingly, one like Jessie into magazine-attractiveness, but otherwise they do not much bother with the imaginative revision or re-creation of what they see. We remember Theo Grote's remark, during his proposal to Belinda, that beauty does not matter to him. These men do not seem very interested in, or curious about, the opposite sex as a whole. On the other hand, the women Pym presents typically imagine men to be basically different from themselves. They see men as a class with greater vulnerabilities and different, more important needs than their own, and usually rush to fill the needs they have themselves created. From Harriet's continual concern to feed Mr. Donne well, to Mildred's fantasy of Everard lying sick and unattended, to the womanly declaration that men need eggs—the feminine imagination in these novels is awfully busy creating Man, a being superior to, but more vulnerable than, women.

Perceiving men as needier and more important than themselves, these women often define their purpose from their idea of male needs, as is the case with Jane and Mildred. Both women think in terms of the "burden" they will or should carry for a man, though for Mildred this attitude is an adjunct of her stance toward all others. Even so, the concept of responding to the needs of others in any form is foreign to the majority of Pym's men in the earlier novels, none of whom are do-gooders at large or aware of the needs of women in particular or in general. They think, instead, of their own needs, assume that women will satisfy them, or, at the least, that women will ease their burden. Without especially thinking about it, women sacrifice their own interests to men, as Flora does when she develops an interest in geography for the sake of her boyfriend, and as her mother did when she started imagining herself as "the clergyman's wife." For Jane, assuming the primary importance of Nicholas's occupation means failing to fulfill the promise of her own talents. This is to be expected: women and not men are the helpmates whose role dictates their supportive participation in another's fulfillment.

Since their need to love is a primary motivation for women, some of them are amazingly assertive in attaining it, especially when it comes to marriage. The quiet Mildred is as determined as the confident Allegra in this regard. Agatha and Olivia Berridge kindly propose to men too modest to offer themselves, and we are led to believe that Jessie arranges Fabian according to her wishes because Nicholas reports, moments before the engagement is discovered, that Fabian had told him a few days since "that he was not thinking of marrying again." Some women, like Belinda, are content with their passivity, but others risk the onus of rejection. In these novels, pursuit for the sake of love belongs to women. Men pursue women, when they do, for primarily practical reasons. Everard Bone is no different in this regard from Theo Grote or Mr. Mold; the bishop and the librarian want a woman to help them into the grave, and the anthropologist wants an indexer and proofreader. We can applaud the assertion of the women who go after what they want, but we cannot claim it as a similarity between the sexes: women's pursuit of satisfaction for their need to love only emphasizes their great difference from men. In Pym's first novels, "women like to have something to dote on," but men believe that "Love is only one of many passions and it has no great influence on the sum of life."

Pym's growing awareness that the emotional lives of men and women are not altogether different in kind is expressed in minor characters and in the unsuccessful ones that figure in *Crampton Hodnet*. Count Bianco is as romantically inclined as Belinda or Harriet Bede and, like them, thrives on an impossible love. Connie Aspinall marries from considerations as practical as those that prompt Theo to propose to her, and she is delighted with her fate. Francis Cleveland longs so deeply for romantic love that he decides to risk his appreciable comforts in order to be with Barbara Bird. Stephen Latimer learns the difference between proposing a safe marriage for practical considerations and falling in love. And Margaret Cleveland is totally uninterested in romantic love. In her early novels, Pym comes closest in *Crampton Hodnet* to expressing the realization that men and women share common needs, problems, and failures. But Margaret's vacuity and Francis's spite and foolish vanity in the particulars of his involvement with Barbara, make it impossible for the reader to take them very seriously—Pym is not sure she takes them seriously, either.

Pym's confidence in the universality of her vision develops and finds expression more gradually in William Caldicote, content to be an observer of life and to feed the pigeons; in Eleanor Hitchins, quite happy, like Everard Bone, Mold, or Parnell, to focus primarily on her career; and in Geoffrey Manifold, awkwardly trying to cheer up the despondent

Prudence. Finally, there are Prudence and Fabian. Though he, being on the verge of marriage, seems to succeed in love while she fails, such is not the case. The woman who believes she must suffer and the man who believes he must hurt women share a common failing: their self-centeredness makes it impossible for them to make a genuine commitment to another. This basic similarity between fully realized characters signals Pym's readiness to explore the minds and hearts of men.

III. Women, Men, and Affirmations

With *Less Than Angels*, Pym begins to extend her vision
to include men as full citizens of the emotional life. It is no
longer a matter, in the next four novels we shall consider, of
women seeming to have one nature and men another; the
two camps divided according to gender in the earlier novels
give way to a more homogeneous and humane picture. Men
and women experience the same problems and confront the
same choices; they have the same needs, are capable of the
same strengths, and are subject to the same failings. Tom,
the central character of *Less Than Angels*, is an anthropologist made to face the question of whether he will observe life
or participate in it; the same choice that disturbed Mildred
Lathbury (*EW*) confronts Tom, and the question reveals its
ultimacy by its effect on a personality very different from
Mildred's. Harry Talbot and Rodney Forsyth, in *A Glass of
Blessings*, feel the need for love and romance as keenly as
Belinda and Harriet Bede (*STG*), while Keith aspires to be
useful to, and needed by, his lover with the zeal of Jane
Cleveland (*JP*), but with greater success. In *No Fond Return of
Love*, Aylwin Forbes is not introduced as a person who is
already, for reasons Pym does not disclose, in love with
someone unsuitable, like Belinda or Harriet; he is more like
Prudence Bates (*JP*), a person whose imagined self demands
that he seek out inappropriate choices, and who prides himself on his romantic role. Finally, one of Pym's most appealing men is Rupert Stonebird of *An Unsuitable Attachment*. As
excellent in his way as Mildred Lathbury is in hers, he also
finds his emotional focal point by responding to the need he
perceives in another.

In order to indicate the outline of my view of Pym's treatment of men, I have thus far ignored the women, many of
whom figure more importantly than the abovementioned
men in these novels. The commentary will correct this imbalance, for Pym's awareness that she treats universal topics
is underlined by her presentation of female and male characters with parallel traits, inclinations, or problems in each

novel. Of course, some difficulties that have traditionally belonged to women or to men continue to trouble them primarily—it is easier, for instance, for the woman who wants to keep her distance from the world to do so if she has a husband like Rodney Forsyth. But retirement enables Alaric Lydgate to do the same thing. It is easier, also, for a man like Tom, upon whom there is no social pressure to live a "full life" (in the sense of acquiring a wife), to persuade himself that he is married to his work and disappear into darkest Africa. But the ability to withdraw into work also tempts Catherine. All of this makes it sound, I fear, as if Pym wrote about a dreary asexual bunch flinching beneath the same weighty problems, the sort of people none of us would wish to know. The truth is quite different: the novels are "affirmations" because, one way or another, women and men (with one notable exception) find fulfillment that nourishes their emotional lives.

Less Than Angels

In *Less Than Angels*, the novelist gives Catherine Oliphant most of her attention, but Tom Mallow, the anthropologist who is Catherine's lover, is central. The novel opens shortly before Tom comes home from the field and ends shortly after his death in Africa. It is Tom, through his profession and his romantic affairs, who links the "bohemian" life of Catherine, the anthropologists' circle that gathers around the new research center, the suburban community of anthropology student Deirdre Swan, and the country life in Shropshire, where Tom's family and Elaine, his first love, still live. There are many characters in this novel, but they and their communities are fully realized and integrated in two smoothly intertwined plotlines: the competition of three women for Tom's heart and the competition, among four students, for research grants. A third (and hidden) conflict involves the competition between Felix Mainwaring and Egidio Gemini for Minnie Foresight's money. The novel is about the uses, pleasures, and dangers of observation, and some of the themes that elucidate this subject are observation versus participation, alienation or detribalization (referring specifically to characters who lack or have lost association with their tribes or tribal customs), loneliness, and the processing of life by fiction and by the study of anthropology.

In a book full of characters happily observing as much of each other as is more or less consistent with decency and decorum, Pym gives Catherine Oliphant and Tom Mallow professions that necessarily make them to some extent observers of life and people. Tom, a twenty-nine-year-old anthropologist, writes his Ph.D. thesis in the course of the novel, based on almost two years of observing "his tribe" in Africa. (Pym is writing in the days before the "disappearing subject" was a problem.) When he tells a layperson that an anthropologist must be detached, an officious acquaintance adds, quoting from a manual, that "no expression of disgust, astonishment or amusement must show on the face of the investigator." Catherine, who thinks she looks like Jane Eyre, is a thirty-one-year-old writer of women's magazine fiction and articles. Since her inspiration comes from everyday life, she has, like Tom, a quasi-official license as an observer of others.

But there is a difference in the lovers' approach to, and use of, their living material. The expressions prohibited by the anthropologists' manual suggest the superiority and distance sometimes assumed by the observer of a "primitive" people. Moreover, the observer's deadpan is translated into enbalmed prose. Thinking of the African festivals he has watched, Tom remembers writing them up,

> avoiding in his descriptions the least suggestion of vivid or picturesque language, and flattening out the whole thing until it sounded rather less interesting than a flower show and carnival in a small English market town. (177)

Catherine, perhaps because she does not observe people who seem remote from herself, believes that life is "sometimes too strong and raw and must be made palatable by fancy." She knows that life is not like the romantic fictions she writes, in which men are impossibly handsome, conversation bookishly romantic, and endings idiotically blissful. Once, when she reads a bit of Tom's thesis, she concludes disdainfully that scholars are cowards who observe superficialities and shrink back from the province of poets and novelists, analyses of the human heart, mind, and soul. In spite of her different material, Catherine's work also creates and keeps a distance from the world she observes, though she does not realize it. Pym gives us a delightful image for her profession in her mincing machine, "Beatrice, a strangely gentle and gracious name for the fierce little iron contraption whose strong teeth so ruthlessly pounded up meat and gristle." Catherine's romantic fiction does the same with life: it takes what she believes is raw, grim, or, even worse, ordinary, and makes it into something agreeable or even interesting. Tom's writing, on the other hand, takes what might be colorful or exotic and squeezes it into the dry bones he needs for his objective scholarly soup.

The differences between the pair's work reflect temperamental differences that affect their relationship and surface in their breakup. Tom has broken away from his solid country background and a host of relatives to pursue a life and career they consider strange and déclassé. He entered into a live-in relationship with Catherine casually, because it suited his needs when he had nowhere to stay in London. This self-sufficient woman, having no tribe of her own, envies Tom the one he has rejected, and would like to acquire all those relatives, along with some children, through marriage. But though Tom returns as a matter of course to live in her apartment after almost two years away, and though their relationship is as dull, according to her, as if they were married, he never thinks of matrimony. Catherine's sense of the superiority of her gender is implicit in her notion that many men (including Tom) are like children who want to be told what to do, or like "trusting animals" who expect to be fed and otherwise cared for. Neither her lover, with his experience in the field far from the comforts of homey women, nor any other man in the novel causes her to revise her estimate. However, just as Catherine assumes her superiority by virtue of her understanding and maturity, Tom assumes his by reason of his gender and his "serious" (academic) work. Though this underlying conflict remains unspoken between them, it expresses itself in Tom's disloyalty.

As we first see in the breakup between him and Catherine, Tom's detachment goes beyond the absence of prejudice or bias so important to the investigator, extending into his personal life as aloofness and insensitivity. Other anthropologists might be "broadened" by learning through their field work of the differences or underlying similarities among all peoples; Tom's studies have added perverse curlicues to his selfishness. After expressing his interest in another woman, for example, he starts to tell Catherine that polygamy is a far better arrangement than monogamy. Later, he reflects that relationships with women like her, who have no "kinship ties," are "better" than others because they are easier for a man to end. Catherine, in contrast to Tom's genuine aloofness, only seems detached. When she sees him holding hands with Deirdre Swan in what had been "their" restaurant, she immediately decides their relationship is over and naturally assumes he must leave her apartment. Before she can confront him with a composed face and attitude, she feels shaken and terribly alone, experiencing the need for community. Since she has no close friends and knows no excellent woman to whom she can turn for comfort, the best she can do for human help in her "nightmare" is to walk into a huge restaurant and sit listening to the talk around her.

A degree of detachment returns when she realizes that perhaps the Greek restaurant was simply a place she and Tom frequented because it was cheap and convenient. By the time he saunters into her flat, she seems entirely detached. There are no reproaches for his betrayal, no scenes before or after she helps him break his news. She manages to sustain this attitude for almost two weeks—until it is convenient for Tom to leave her apartment. The closest she comes to taking a well-deserved shot at him is when she remarks,

> It seems rather cold-blooded, doesn't it, not going for a week or two? In books and films and even in life, too, people go and pack suit-cases there and then and hurry out of the house. (115)

Tom is much too tired from walking with Deirdre to deal with all of that. Ironically, he cries before he eventually goes and implies that it is she who is cold-hearted: "I suppose you'll write an article called 'After he's gone,' and make use of all this." She agrees that it "might be a good title" and cries— after he's gone. Tom correctly assumes that Catherine can withdraw into her work almost at will, but he is wrong to believe that her ability means the absence of emotion.

Tom is willing that Catherine should think their life together is over because of Deirdre, a nineteen-year-old student of anthropology who fell in love with him at first sight in the research center. "She needs me," he says simply, as if he intended somehow (and without previous experience) to become a supportive man. In fact, he turned to the girl from largely unacknowledged dissatisfactions with Catherine because she no longer serves *his* needs. Whereas Deirdre is "still young enough to be moulded," according to a friend, Catherine is "too much of a personality in her own right," according to Tom. He complains that she tried to make him into her idea of what he should be, but the real problem is that she no longer conforms to his idea of what she should be in the "reciprocal relationship—the woman giving the food and the shelter and doing some typing for him and the man giving the priceless gift of himself."

Nor is Tom alone in his expectations. Some former students who hang out in the college department of anthropology, Pym tells us,

> had been fortunate enough to win the love of devoted women—women who might one day become their wives, but who, if they were thrown aside, would accept their fate cheerfully and without bitterness. They had learned early in life what it is to bear love's burdens, listening patiently to their men's troubles and ever ready at their typewriters, should a manuscript or even a short article get to the stage of being written down. (49)

Catherine is too busy with her own work to spend time with Tom at his leisure or to type up his work. She is occasionally silly or satirical and he dislikes being taken less than seriously or being criticized (however mildly). When Tom wants admiration and sympathy, which Deirdre provides, Catherine expects him to be mature about the work he has chosen to do. She is perhaps too mature about this. At a critical point, when Tom feels he has "lost faith" in the value of his dissertation and of anthropology, she cannot help except by quoting Matthew Arnold, which most people probably would not consider helpful. Hearing "Ah, love, let us be true to one another," Tom imagines not encouragement but an accusation for his growing interest in Deirdre, who has no doubt of the importance of his work. But he also realizes, during his crisis, that Catherine never even tried to understand anthropology. This did not matter before, but now he sees it as her cardinal sin: she did not pretend to make his interests her own.

With Deirdre, his inferior in age and experience, Tom expects no complications. She lives in the suburbs surrounded by her family and an entire community, a whole tribe from whom she longs to escape and whose Sunday customs Jean-Pierre le Rossignol, a French student of anthropology and friend of Deirdre's, comes to observe. Her brother Malcolm is a normally dull young man, but her widowed mother, Mabel Swan, and her unmarried aunt, Rhoda Wellcome, are one of Pym's feminine pairs, living together in comfortable affection enlivened by a few set rivalries and minor irritations. The women are themselves notable observers, especially Rhoda, whose particular subject is Alaric Lydgate, their neighbor. From upstairs windows, she observes his strange actions in the next-door garden with no detachment at all, but with as much interest as if he were the sole survivor of some outlandish tribe.

About love, Deirdre has drearily conventional ideas: a man needs a woman who understands him, a woman who can share his interests and work, and love means a totally uncritical acceptance. About the relationship between Tom and Catherine, she feels no compunctions. She thinks they do not behave publicly as if they are in love, believes that a man must grow tired of a woman who is "neither particularly beautiful nor even young," reasons that women who are no longer very young do not suffer much (especially if they have other interests), and concludes that Catherine is very strong and cares only about her writing anyhow. Deirdre combines the ruthlessness of happy love and youth perfectly, but, as we watch her frantic efforts to hold Tom to herself, it is impossible to dislike her. From the frequent difficulty she experiences in knowing what to say to him to her fear that he does not like her haircut, she is in a continual welter of anxiety.

In Tom's relationship with Deirdre, which he is able to control to his own satisfaction, and in his visit to his family, his detachment and his confusion of "the field" and his own life are evident. He hesitates about dining at his girlfriend's house because, unlike Catherine, she has "kinship ties" that might entail repercussions. One imagines Mabel, Rhoda, and Malcolm on the rampage, vandalizing Tom's scholarly notes, perhaps, if he trifles with Deirdre. Walking by the river close to her home, he identifies it as "the place where the young men and women walk at night and are allowed a certain amount of license"—and hastens to behave as local convention dictates. When she declares her love, no expression of disgust, astonishment, or amusement shows on his face as he thinks about the fears and strategies of women in general. There is no answering declaration. He sees her only "as often as . . . necessary for his well-being and happiness." Though that is not as often as she would like, it is the schedule he requires as he writes his thesis.

With his own family, Tom's detachment wavers very little. He thinks when he hears about a cousin's debutante ball that it is as primitive a ceremony as any he has observed, and a flower show at home, in Shropshire, reminds him of African festivals he has attended. These things might not be important, but he feels distant from the occasions and people surrounding him. Although Tom is present, he does not participate, as Pym suggests in the scene where he goes to his cousin's house on the night of the ball. He stands outside in his scruffy attire, wondering, "Was it just his clothes, then, that were keeping him out of paradise? It must be something more than that." A friendly policeman, who cannot believe that Tom's aunt lives there, suggests that he go on his way. His brother's study, decorated with animal prints and stuffed animal heads, makes him feel "as if he were observing some aspect of a culture as alien to him as any he had seen in Africa." Although we recognize that his condition is appalling in itself, it is hard to feel much sympathy for a man whose malaise makes him complacent, unfeeling, self-centered, and manipulative.

Though Tom's detachment has dessicated his personal life, Pym does not suggest that he represents anthropologists in general. Most of the people who gather around the research center are comfortably human, laughing, chatting, gossiping (with no objectivity), and generally carrying on like people anywhere. Several stand out in this well-drawn circle. Esther Clovis, whom we already know, having resigned her position at the Learned Society, is her competent self as the quasi-manager of the research center. A couple of times, she mentions Everard and Mildred Bone ("a rather dull woman") and their field work in Africa. She lives now in close if occasionally brusque friendship with Gertrude Lydgate, a specialist in languages. Esther seems softer than in *Excellent Women*, as she grows sentimental over young people in general and over memories of a man who made a pass at her many years ago. Egidio Gemini, a friend of Gertrude's because he is also a linguistics expert, is a Roman Catholic priest of unspecified order and musty black robes. Mark Penfold, Digby Fox, Vanessa Eaves, and Primrose Cutbush are different personalities but as competitive and serious about their work as advanced students anywhere.

Among the other anthropologists, Alaric Lydgate and Felix Mainwaring especially claim our interest because they shed light on Tom. Alaric, a man somewhere in middle age, feels truly detribalized. Back in England after being invalided out of the Colonial Service, he spent eleven years living among "Tom's tribe." He is not exactly an anthropologist since he has not yet written anything from the trunks of notes moldering in his attic. He cannot produce his own work, so he enjoys writing scathing reviews of others' efforts. As he observes the labor of others, his favorite phrase is "It is a pity," as in "It is a pity . . . that the author did not take the trouble to inform himself of some of the elementary facts." Sometimes he wears a horrific African mask as he sits alone, "withdrawing himself from the world":

> He often thought what a good thing it would be if the wearing of masks or animals' heads could become customary for persons over a certain age. How restful social intercourse would be if the face did not have to assume any expression—the strained look of interest, the simulated delight or surprise, the anxious concern one didn't really feel. Alaric often avoided looking into people's eyes when he spoke to them, fearful of what he might see there, for life was very terrible whatever sort of front we might put on it. (57)

Clearly, Alaric is infected by the disease running amok in Tom: detachment as a release from feeling and social intercourse. But his fearfulness and vulnerability make his case different. Without the mask, he feels exposed and "defenceless," yet he is very lonely, with only his sister Gertrude and Esther Clovis as occasional visitors. He observes the Swan family next door with as much interest as the sisters accord him, but with a pathetic wistfulness. Obviously, Alaric is not really content to wear the stifling expressionless mask.

Like Tom, Felix Mainwaring chose to detribalize himself by selecting anthropology over the more conventional career and life indicated by his background. Felix is a good-looking old man and a snob toward his colleagues. He has no real interest in anthropology anymore, but relishes the exercise of his charm on women like Minnie Foresight to get money for such things as the research center and research grants. He squires her about and sweet-talks her—for the sake of anthropology. "*Floreat scientia!*" as Esther Clovis says. Mainwaring is an avatar of the self-centered man who extracts support for his own ends from women. Just as he gets money from Mrs. Foresight, loses some, and finds a new source, Tom gets emotional and practical support from Catherine, eventually finds it insufficient, and turns to Deirdre. Felix loses some of his silvery luster over the Foresight grants, which Minnie has promised to fund. The serviceable Miss Clovis eventually has to announce that there will be no grants. Father Gemini (whose coworker is Father Serpentelli) swiped the money for his own research. Felix promises more than he delivers.

The competition for the Foresight grants parallels the competition for Tom, which is primarily in his and Deirdre's minds. Catherine may miss him, but it is he who calls her from time to time, like the evening he finishes his thesis and proposes an immediate celebration. She puts him off. For a moment, he is sad to learn that she has already bought a bottle of wine for this occasion, but the moment passes. He is confused by his persistent but unresolved feelings about her: "I think I was in love with her in a curious way and perhaps still am," he tells his mother. Deirdre should fear his feelings about Catherine; instead, her insecurities focus on Elaine, the old friend in Shropshire who was Tom's first love. Pym's description of her is concise but complete. The eldest daughter who stayed home while her two younger sisters prepared for careers, she comes from a good country family with money. Elaine has created a whole life around "her country activities, the dogs, the garden, the women's institute, the church work"; she has disciplined herself not to think of Tom.

When Tom arrives to visit his family, he is still confused about his work as an anthropologist, wondering, as he had told Catherine, whether it would have been better, more useful, to have stayed at home: "What's the use of it all. Who will benefit from my work, what exactly is the *point* of my researches?" To this turmoil created by the need somehow to matter to others is added confusion about Elaine. Though he notices that she is "sharp," or critical, like Catherine, he sees her as the perfect companion, and when she asks if he is attached, he says he is married only to his work. He is led to a degree of self-awareness as they reminisce, perhaps because he is so comfortable with her:

> He found himself mourning the young man of those days, who went for long country walks and quoted poetry. Now he went into Regent's Park and talked about his thesis. He wondered if the change was for the better. (185)

Tom is in trouble because Elaine reminds him of a different self. From his brief remarks to Catherine about his "lost faith," which were deflected by her incomprehension and his dissatisfaction with her, Tom's questions have grown larger, involving not so much anthropology as the kind of man he has become, a detached observer who feels nowhere as if he belongs.

But by the time he returns to London, he has covered the real issue of what sort of man he wants to be, with the question of what to do about the women in his life. Like the child Catherine thinks he resembles, he expects her, of all people, to advise him about Elaine. After she refuses to instruct him, he says he is returning to Africa and provokes Catherine's scorn:

> How soothing it will be to get away from all this complexity of personal relationships to the simplicity of a primitive tribe, whose only complications are in their kinship structure and

73

rules of land tenure, which you can observe with the anthropologist's calm detachment. (186)

She is correct in her assumptions about his motives. Even
Digby realizes that Tom's trip home accounts, somehow, for
his rushing back to Africa needlessly, and his intuition tells
him that Tom has realized his alienation from his family and
their useful lives. Running away from his perplexities about
himself, from the messy difficulty of sorting out what and
whom he wants for himself, Tom runs away from life. And,
of course, his choice of detached observation earns him the
fate of the proverbial cat. The parallel to the Foresight competition holds to the end. Just as there are no grants, so
there is no prize in the competition for Tom Mallow.

Curiously, as if Pym means to suggest that losing Tom is
losing nothing, his "survivors" all gain something in the af-
termath of his death. At the tea organized by his sister, she,
Elaine, Deirdre, and Catherine sip sherry decorously while
discussing what to do with Tom's notes, the dry bones of his
efforts. (No one really wants them.) "We represent all the
different aspects of [Tom's] life," says Catherine, and we
think of the almost archetypal roll call, beginning with his
sister and running through his subsequent loves: the comfortable girl next door, the woman who loved him and moth-
ered him, and the adoring girl toward whom he felt vaguely
protective and very superior. Elaine, the stickler, will continue her full and useful country life, consoled, surely, by
being the official "widow" since Tom left an unfinished letter
to her. Deirdre, the clinger, finds love by Tom's death. Digby,
who has been biding his time, gets Tom's girl as well as the
unused portion of his grant money. Unhappily for Deirdre,
this means exchanging one lover in Africa for another lover
in Africa.

But Catherine, the detribalized rescuer of men in need,
gains the most. First, she replaces the cowardly man running
away from emotional difficulty with a heroic figure who died
helping an oppressed people fight for freedom, an outstanding example of her fictionalizing abilities. When she goes to
Mabel Swan and Rhoda Wellcome in her grief, she is adopted
by the tribe, who coddle and console her. She withdraws
into their safe haven for almost two weeks, but finally needs

her own life again and returns home. She particularly wants to do this in order to nurture an interest that has been growing since before Tom's departure: the lonely and attractive Alaric Lydgate is another man who needs rescuing. When Catherine first met him, across the garden hedge at the Swan house, she found him intriguing and attractive, and eventually she turned him into a big-game hunter for one of her stories.

The relationship has grown by the time she comes to stay next door. Significantly for a Jane Eyre look-alike, she decides he's like Mr. Rochester, though he is enslaved by the trunks of notes in his attic rather than by a mad wife. Catherine suggests that he free himself of the burden by burning them, and he does, in a great bonfire that is most appropriate on Guy Fawkes Night. We see them for the last time from the vantage point of Rhoda and Mabel's house—how "comfortable it sometimes was to observe [life] from a distance, to look down from an upper window, as it were, as the anthropologists did." Alaric brandishes a knife, cutting rhubarb and filling Catherine's arms with it, as if he were paying homage to the minor English goddess who liberated him from his mask and his notes, from his fearful detachment, into the life of a man.

Observation of our fellow creatures is one of the great pleasures of life, but in Tom Mallow, Pym explores its dangers. For Tom, the question of whether to observe or participate in life is complicated by his habit of detachment, as it was not for Mildred Lathbury. She cared for the people she observed and participated (too much) in their troubles. Tom is a failure because feeling, as she did, the urge to participate, he flees his own humanity. Catherine cultivates detachment to counter what she considers an excess of feeling, but her observation does not preclude participation. As Tom confuses his life with the field, Catherine confuses hers with fiction. However, her confusion is not alienating, like Tom's: Jane Eyre must help Mr. Rochester. All of Pym's characters here are "less than angels": the sneaky, maneuvering Father Gemini, the oily, charming Felix, and the mean-spirited Mark are only the most obvious examples. But when Tom chooses the soulless existence of a bull or a bear, his choice makes him less than human.

The question of which is the stronger sex or which is the more vulnerable (is the loneliness of men more pathetic than that of women?) is raised by Catherine when Tom says Deirdre needs him. Other characters, especially Digby, ask the same question, though often jokingly, and Pym answers it with the complexity it deserves. Catherine has always imagined her husband will be "a strong character who would rule her life." However, as we remarked, she considers most men, including Tom and Alaric, children. Though it is a simplification, she is correct about Tom, who is too weak to face his own troubles. But she is not right about Alaric. She feels so responsible for him only because she does not appreciate the courage and strength it takes for him to burn his notes.

Though not as important or as old as Alaric, Digby also shows signs of strength. He is remarkably patient waiting for Deirdre to turn to him. As Catherine remarks when Tom leaves, he capably assumes "the role of comforter, which is often regarded as a kind of female monopoly though it can be admirably filled by the right kind of man." Digby's romantic interest does not lessen the quality of the persistence and patience with which he waits until Deirdre "needs" him. These characteristics we associate more readily with women in fiction than with young men: Catherine herself is only one of Pym's women who need to feel needed by the men in their lives. She and Elaine show considerable strength.

Both have built an image of themselves as strong, contented, well able to manage and—more than to survive—to live fully. Though some men, like Tom, and some women, like the immature Deirdre, are pleased that it should be so because it enables them to act with no consideration or guilt, their superficiality cannot diminish the women's achievement of strength and dignity. Pym's treatment of these characters implies that the question of which is the stronger sex is meaningless.

A Glass of Blessings

Pym's characters often remind us that, in a love relationship, we want the pleasure of being able to give a lover something which, but for us, he would lack. What we give first and always is the gift of ourselves, and in giving that, we each have a unique ability to give precisely what our lovers desire. All the time, however, this seemingly simple matter is liable to complication by any number of factors—by familiarity, by one partner's assumption of inequality, or by the nature of the "gift" he requires, to mention only three. Everard Bone (*EW*) wants, for instance, someone to do some typing and an index. Esther Clovis could and might do it, but he wants Mildred Lathbury to do the work. The question of whether he wants her to serve his needs because she appeals to him or whether she appeals to him because she might be willing to serve his needs is impossible to answer. But Mildred, who is attracted to him, is willing to give the mundane something he requires (which is, after all, a sign of her potential devotion to him and his interests), and from this gift, presumably, deep affection blossoms and leads to marriage. She has in the meantime the pleasures of deciding whether she will carry the burden and of telling herself that Everard needs her.

This desire to be needed, to have a particular purpose of some kind in relation to others, extends beyond romantic love and is central to *A Glass of Blessings*. The novel deals with a search for purpose and community that ends in success and renewal for Wilmet Forsyth, the narrator of the story. As Wilmet tries to find a particular context and way in which she might feel useful or necessary, Pym presents male characters whose emotional needs parallel Wilmet's. She might be Mrs. Magoo when it comes to the needs and feelings of the people around her: at first, she fails entirely to see the similarities linking her to women and men she often considers unattractive. But Pym insists, through the parallels, that men and women are moved by identical needs, disquieted by similar yearnings. The novel is about Wilmet's education as she learns about herself, other women, men, and love—about her development as a mature woman by initiation into what she calls "different worlds." Some of the novel's themes, then, are the need for usefulness or purpose, detachment and engagement, the need for community, the emotional similarities of the sexes, the ubiquity of romance, and the tedium or blessings of familiarity.

Wilmet is bored with her marriage and lacks other interests that might compensate for the romance she misses. She does not have a demanding old mother to look after, like Mary Beamish; she cannot have children, so she does not have a family to raise and a household to run, like her friend Rowena Talbot; and she does not have a career. What she has is Rodney, a husband who thinks married women should not work unless the money is needed, and a mother-in-law, Sybil Forsyth, an amusing and independent woman with many interests and activities. Since the young Forsyths live in Sybil's elegant London house, Wilmet lives like a pampered child in another woman's domain, where she does nothing more than arrange flowers occasionally. We discover, as her pleasant voice makes her life known to us, that Wilmet is an attractive snob, scrupulously attentive to her clothes.

In a world where women have their work in the home or elsewhere, she feels as useless as the Faberge egg Father Thames keeps in his study. Beauty may be the egg's only reason for being, but Wilmet suspects that more might reasonably be expected of a woman. She would not feel so guilty if women everywhere and in a variety of ways were not so capably putting their talents to some purpose. Mary Beamish, an unmarried woman in her early thirties, is irredeemably dowdy from Wilmet's point of view, but looks after her demanding, ailing mother and does innumerable good works in the church and community. Sybil, who is an agnostic, gathers old clothes for poor parishes and does what Wilmet calls "social work," serving on local committees for good causes. A strange lady refuses to wait in line at the blood bank because she is R-negative: "Why somebody might be dying for want of my blood while I sat here waiting!" Obviously, she is well convinced of the need for what she contributes, and many women and men are no different. Sybil remarks one day, of a priest with a "good" name and a parish at a bad address, "There is still that ideal of service among the nobly born," but Bill Coleman, master of ceremonies at St. Luke's, and Father Bode, whom no one would ever accuse of noble birth, are moved by the same ideal.

Men and women together compose what Wilmet calls "the burden-bearing type," a class that seems a personal reproach to herself though it has no appeal for her.

Essentially, Wilmet likes her idleness as her husband's status symbol; otherwise, she would challenge Rodney or plunge more readily into the good causes that keep Mary Beamish or Sybil so busily purposeful. Instead, she imagines how cozy it would be to work in an office with other women, banding together to defy the boss with "insolent detachment": the sniping in the skirmish of the sexes has not ended though the work of men and women is no longer defined according to sex. Wilfred Bason, whom Wilmet and Rodney lead to the job at the clergy house, and who preens himself on his cooking, is more house-proud and fastidious than Mrs. Greenhill, who preceded him as housekeeper. Wilfred asserts that women do not understand the "finer points of cooking" with the canard that the greatest chefs have all been men. Then there are the "splendid and formidable women" who pursue careers in traditional male occupations, like Eleanor Hitchens (*JP*), and "the ones who carry [shopping] baskets as well as briefcases," the married career women. Eleanor is a civil servant like Rodney, at the same ministry, but though he does not deny her competence, he suggests that she is unfeminine. According to Sybil, Rodney fears Wilmet would become a similarly "formidable" woman if she worked. He might be right. It is certain that if she gave to work half the concentration she devotes to her costumes, she could succeed at almost anything. But Rodney does not go as far as Piers Longridge, who remarks at a dinner party, "Intellectual women are seldom attractive. . . . The combination of beauty with brains is to me unnatural and therefore repellent." Based on personal experience, Rodney knows that beautiful and brainy women are not always intimidating or repellent. (Since brains are attributed only to women who work outside of the home, he does not mean Wilmet.) Rodney has met an intelligent *and* attractive woman who works for Arthur Grampian and broke off an engagement to a member of Parliament. Sybil, who continually twits her son and others about their old-fashioned ideas regarding women, wonders whether Prudence Bates "was too beautiful to be an M.P.'s wife" or whether Edward Lyall was "too stupid to be the husband of an intelligent woman."

Wilmet inevitably feels out of step in this world of busy people, all needed at their respective tasks, and she is resolved to find the place and way in which she too can have a purposeful life. Given limitations that she feels are imposed, most unfairly, by her money, class, and family situation, she focuses her efforts on two fronts: the church and Piers Longridge, the attractive brother of her good friend Rowena. Naturally, she fails to see the irony in her simultaneous efforts to draw closer to the church and to launch an extramarital romance. Wilmet turns to St. Luke's from a need for community, for a place where she belongs, in her own right, with people of a common faith and interests. Her only friend when the novel begins is Rowena Talbot. With this chum, she can reminisce about their youthful infatuation as Wrens with Rocky Napier (*EW*), or she can share a laugh about the "far-fetched situation" of a magazine story written by Catherine Oliphant (*LTA*), in which a woman sees her lover holding hands with a girl at a Greek restaurant. But Rowena lives in the country with her husband and children, so Sybil is Wilmet's only real companion.

Sybil is "a real character," according to Wilmet, and often entertaining company, as when she reads book titles without her glasses: "Victory Over Pan" and "My Tears at the Vatican" sound like good reads. She draws Wilmet out somewhat, talking her into restaurants where the fastidious young woman does not dare examine the lettuce and suggesting they take an evening class in Portuguese, taught by Piers. But the trouble is that she has her friends, her community, and they are not Wilmet's.

Regrettably, really good people are often not really fun people; understandably, Wilmet's efforts to enter the world of the church are marked by a deep ambivalence. Though she goes to services and social functions at St. Luke's, she believes she is different from her fellow parishioners and resists them. The large world she divides into the circle of martini drinkers, to which she belongs, and the different circle of tea drinkers, into which she thinks she is being initiated at the church. Her classification conjures up two distinct images, and there is no doubt that she feels the tea drinkers, as a group, tend to be unattractive and "slightly common." Reflecting on the friendship of Miss Prideaux and Sir Denbigh, Wilmet realizes that the need for a sustaining common ground with others transcends social differences, but does not realize that this observation has anything to do with her own situation. Father Bode, whom everyone agrees is a good man, she sees as tacky, dumpy, and much too earnest in a low-class way. When Mary Beamish makes friendly overtures, Wilmet tries to deflect them by emphasizing their differences, going out of her way to make herself seem even more frivolous than she is in reality; the woman whose good works shame her is just "not [her] kind of person."

Wilmet has a marked tendency to detachment, in spite of her desire to establish a connection with the people at St. Luke's. Her ambivalence is also reflected in her imagination. On the one hand, it has its sympathetic side, which finds pathos in such things as her fantasy that a plain and aged office worker has deprived herself to buy pussywillows for her dingy office. On the other hand, her imagination has its alienating aspect. There is a good dollop of patronage in her notion that her elegance disturbs unattractive women. More often than this, her imagination produces maliciously funny visions of others: Mary mentions that her mother likes meat for dinner and Wilmet sees Mrs. Beamish "crouching greedily over a great steak."

St. Luke's represents a very different world from the one to which she is accustomed. Wilmet expects the attention and deference of men. But in the church, a couple of men seem unimpressed by her good looks and act mildly hostile when she interrupts their conversation. She anticipates that Marius Ransome, the handsome assistant priest, will find her attractive and single her out since he is definitely "her" kind. But, apart from exchanging a few sympathetic glances with her, he does nothing of the sort. When the thought crosses her mind that Mary might be interested in Marius, she dismisses it as the "classic situation" of plain spinster enamored of handsome and inaccessible priest. But she eventually wonders if Marius might exercise his charm on her but not on Mary because he regards the latter as a "fine person" and herself as "less fine"; she does not know the ground rules or the significance of the moves in this new environment.

In the group at the church, Father Thames (who tells Wilmet he cannot abide Indian tea) and Wilfred Bason share her love of beautiful things, but her first experience of theft at close quarters occurs when the housekeeper "borrows" the priest's Faberge egg. By accident, she, who likes to turn away with "womanly delicacy" from anything distasteful, becomes the person to whom the theft is confided by a concerned Bill Coleman. By coincidence, she then runs into Wilfred and persuades him to return the egg secretly, with her help, before it is missed. When she discovers that Father Thames has known of Bason's enterprise all along, and that this is not the first time, she amazedly hears his version of Christian forbearance: "It seems selfish to keep one's possessions too much to oneself, doesn't it, when they can give so much pleasure to others." Certainly, this is a new world for Wilmet, a place where a young woman who might be expected to travel when she comes into money at her mother's death instead goes into a convent to test her vocation, a place where Wilmet's gradual involvement and willingness to help, rather than her obvious attractions, will gain her the acceptance she desires.

During the time that Wilmet is building, almost in spite of herself, ties with the people at St. Luke's, she is also pursuing Piers Longridge. Seriously bored by marriage and her husband, she longs for romantic excitement. Rodney is a civil servant for whom she feels a "bleak and respectable" house is appropriate. She describes him as a stiff-looking but attractive man who is balding "in a rather distinguished way" suitable to his age and position. In addition to his chauvinistic and self-serving attitude about Wilmet's working, his sins include not remarking on her appearance, transferring a sum of money into her bank account as a birthday present, and being her husband. As Wilmet remarks, those little things that initially seem lovable about a person may become a bit tiresome by familiarity. She does not want money, though she recognizes that it is "good and solid." She wants romance.

Rodney may not quiver Wilmet's heart, but he is not as romantically hopeless as she makes him out to be. He is still capable of surprising her with little talents she did not know he possessed (like plumbing). Occasionally, he says things that reveal a man less simple than she believes him to be, as when he remarks cryptically that "we've all of us," at some stage, "loved not wisely but too well." Sometimes he fusses devotedly over her, sometimes he buys her little surprises. But his wife pooh-poohs his small attentions. Those little gifts, she tells herself, are no big deal, since there is always "a good reason" for them: perhaps he sees something in an antique shop window she might like, or perhaps he sees something for which she might once have expressed a liking. In order to feel "admired and cherished," the exigent Wilmet wants Rodney to surprise her "just because it [happens] to be a lovely day." Her ambivalence about her sweetly boring husband is expressed in her thoughts about Harry Talbot, Rowena's husband: strong and reliable men, she believes, are dull but "more comforting to women than the exciting but tortured intellectuals." Flashes of common sense notwithstanding, she craves excitement.

Wilmet's marital boredom and longing for romance are paralleled by Harry Talbot's. As solidly married as Wilmet, he senses in her a restlessness akin to his own and begins a surreptitious courtship. When Wilmet spends the weekend with the Talbots, she is surprised one evening to discover that Harry is holding her hand in the semidarkness of the television—while Rowena smocks a dress contentedly under a lamp in the same room. When he and Wilmet have lunch alone, he is open:

> Now there's a kind of sadness about you that wasn't there before. As if life hadn't turned out quite as you'd hoped it would? . . . I should like us to have fun together—I believe we could. (88–89)

Wilmet laughs off the proposition made by this man she and Rodney have known for ten years, but this experience makes her think, fleetingly, that perhaps Rodney, too, is not as solid and reliable as he appears. But she cannot see her husband as a man with romantic feelings any more than he can see her as a woman who might excite such feelings in others.

After Rowena beautifully defuses the demi-situation with light talk about her husband's anonymous gift to her friend, Wilmet says to Rodney, "It sounds almost as if [Harry] were inviting me to have an affair with him, doesn't it?" Rodney thinks her interpretation is funny.

In spite of bits of proof like Harry's "doggy devotion" to her, Wilmet cannot see that romance is everywhere, blossoming in unlikely hearts and places (even in husbands). Harry, the good spouse and father, anonymously sends her a little enamel box with its provocative message: "If you will not when you may, / When you will you shall have nay." Sybil knits a sweater in a particular shade for Arnold Root, because he has green in his eyes. Professor Root, whom Wilmet considers a nice old bore, sends Sybil two dozen roses with a Greek quotation that figures in a private joke. And he gives the surprised Wilmet a lovely Christmas present that "seems appropriate to your own style of beauty, which, if I may say so, is happily not quite of this age." Romance, to Wilmet, is something that happens to her, an ambiance created by a man who admires and cherishes her, as a husband, by her definition, cannot do. Her own Christmas present to the husband who is "not spontaneous or romantic" is a wallet.

Wilmet can pursue the relationship with Piers for the same reason she can enjoy Harry's attentions. She convinces herself that he needs her to do him some good. Piers is regarded as "unsatisfactory" by his family, according to Wilmet, because he has had a succession of low-level jobs and is unmarried. There is also the possibility that he drinks too much, but generally the feeling is that he has failed to settle down in work and in life. Just as she tells herself she can help Harry see that Rowena is a good wife, she tells herself she might be able to help Piers by her friendship. He is "frustrated and unloved," she tells Sybil, "he needs taking care of." A seductively pure fantasy enables Wilmet to enjoy her flirtations: she will be the woman whose friendly goodness (but not goody-goodness) gently nudges erring (but admiring) men back onto the straight and narrow. In reality, the first time she has lunch with Piers, she learns she has helped him avoid his job as a Portuguese translator.

Her relationship with Piers, though it progresses slowly, assumes a great importance for her, and she is justified in believing that his feelings are as romantic as hers. "I thought we might go for a walk in the park and have tea at a teashop like clandestine lovers," he says the first time he suggests they get together. Later, when she mentions that Rodney is not a jealous man, his flattering rejoinder is, "I should be if you were mine." One evening, he calls in a fit of depression, expecting her to abandon a dinner party in order to keep him company. Though he does not call or see her very often, when he does, he acts like a man falling in love with her, so Wilmet offers herself to him, in her restrained fashion—"if there *was* ever anything I could do":

> I gave myself up to a happy dream in which I went to look after Piers when he was ill or depressed or just had a hangover. And yet, had that been what I meant when I had made my offer to him? Not an offer, exactly. But if not an offer, then what? I felt that Piers really needed me as few people did. Certainly not Rodney, I told myself, justifying my foolish indulgence. Piers needed love and understanding, perhaps already he was happier because of knowing me. (163)

One positive effect of Wilmet's conviction that she is needed is that her sense of kinship to others sprouts a tenuous little bud. Immediately after she leaves Piers, she visits Mary Beamish at the convent she is leaving after discovering she is not right for the life of a nun. Mary has been writing to Marius Ransome, helping him work out his doubts about the Church. "I feel he *needs* me in some way," she says, and Wilmet, feeling "a little bond of happiness" with her, invites her to stay in the Forsyth house while she decides what to do after leaving the convent.

However, in the desire to be needed by Piers, Wilmet has a male counterpart. When Piers invites her to tea at his place, he is inviting her to meet Keith, a handsome young man who sounds "flat" and "common" to Wilmet's refined ears, and who is obviously his lover. Wilmet is in well-bred shock while the domestically talented Keith demonstrates his practical usefulness to Piers. Though she is outraged, naturally her good manners save the situation; besides, her sympathy aroused by the obvious trouble taken on her behalf, she realizes that "it was quite obvious that [she] was going to find it impossible to dislike Keith." But she is still angry with Piers, who denies when they are alone that he misled her. When she tries to figure out *why* Keith, who is a model for knitting magazines (unlike "people one actually *knows*"), Piers counters with scorn and an accusation:

> Not people *you* know, you mean, but there *are* others in the world—in fact quite a few million people outside the narrow select little circle that makes up Wilmet's world. . . . Perhaps I've gone too far. After all I didn't really mean to imply that you're to blame for what you are. Some people are less capable of loving their fellow human beings than others . . . it isn't necessarily their fault. (199)

Once Piers has said these hurtful things, we remember Wilmet's lack of interest and sympathy for others. While wanting to be "lovable" (as she admits to Piers), she has judged a good number of people as unlovable, according to her superficial criteria of age, class, and appearance.

There is enough truth in Piers's remarks to shake Wilmet, who believes "it was no more than [she] deserved for having let [her] thoughts stray to another man." She finds new comfort in the thought of spending time with Mary and going on a parish retreat. As insensitive people imagined Mary Beamish had done when she entered the convent, Wilmet falls back on the Church as her supportive community when romantic love disappoints her. Piers's characterization of her does not, by itself, change Wilmet, whose development is gradual. But her humiliation results in awareness and a loss of confidence that Mary mentions. Wilmet's cursory explanation is that she has discovered she is not "as nice" as she thought she was, but she has also discovered how blinded she was by her critical detachment and self-centeredness. Rowena knew about Piers's homosexuality all along and assumed her friend did, too. Mary and Marius Ransome announce their decision to marry, as do Sybil and Arnold Root, whose plans suggest that age and familiarity are no impediments to love. Right under her powdered nose, Wilmet thinks, these things have been going on without her having been aware of them. Her receptiveness to people she might previously have rejected as not being of her kind is evident when she befriends Keith, whom she likes. She and Rowena decide to tell their husbands only of his job in a coffee bar—the husbands cannot be trusted with the information that Keith is also a model because "men are so narrow-minded and catty."

Since Sybil and Arnold Root want her house to themselves (like any other newlyweds), the search for a place to live throws Wilmet and Rodney together, making her feel they are closer than they have been for years. When they go on an English countryside vacation because Sybil and Arnold want to go to Portugal alone, Wilmet discovers that Rodney too has needs and feelings of the kind with which she never credited him. He sighs for the days of their courtship and says maybe they were "better than [they] shall ever know again," but Wilmet reminds him that "even married life" is "supposed to get better as one grows older." When he confesses that he took Prudence Bates out to dinner "once or twice," perhaps the saddest thing he says is that she reminded him of Wilmet, "rather cool and distant." But after they collapse with laughter about Prudence's uncomfortable Regency sofa, Wilmet has a sober moment:

> I had always regarded Rodney as the kind of man who would never look at another woman. The fact that he could—and has indeed done so—ought to teach me something about myself, even if I was not yet quite sure what it was. (250)

It ought to teach her that her self-involvement has made her dismally unaware of others, and that her yearnings and needs are the same as Rodney's.

Remembering Piers's remarks while she is in Harry Talbot's company, Wilmet concludes that she "might be incapable of loving [her] fellow human beings in a dreary, general way, but [she] could inspire love in others." In fact, though she may not feel a deep affection for mankind in general, she has learned to accept people more readily. In a wonderful scene, she sits in a coffee shop with Rodney, Piers, and Wilf Bason while Keith serves coffee and joins in the talk. Though she is quite at home, perhaps she has not advanced to Piers's rather pretentious idea that we are "all colleagues . . . in this grim business of getting through life as best we can"—but she has had the essential vision of community and of her place and function in it:

> It was both exciting and frightening to think how many differ-
> ent worlds I knew. . . . I could not say that I really *knew* the
> worlds of Piers and Keith, or even of Mr. Coleman and his
> Husky if it came to that. It seemed as if the Church should be
> the place where all worlds could meet, and looking around me
> I saw that in a sense this was so. If people remained outside it
> was our—even *my*—duty to try to bring them in. (209)

She attends the institution of Marius as vicar of a church in the suburbs with a coachload of people from her parish and is very pleased that, at Mary's instigation, she has been initiated into the select circle of women who decorate St. Luke's. The fortunate woman has found a useful place in her house and in her chosen community.

After Wilmet met Keith, she thought about the difference in the meanings of *devout* and *devoted* and considered it "suitable that [her] life should have this confusion in it." Looking for someone to be devoted to her, Wilmet discovers that being devoted to others is part of being devout; seeking romantic excitement and admiration, she discovers the blessings of the ordinary and familiar. The novel, as it draws to a close, mentions "La Cenerentola" a couple of times, and we can identify several Cinderellas among the characters. Father Thames, in his happy translation from an English clergy house to an Italian villa, feels like Cinderella; Sybil and Mary, whom Wilmet saw as impossible candidates, are claimed by their princes; Marius Ransome goes, thanks to the glass slipper of Mary's money, from metaphoric rags to riches; and Wilmet herself, in terms of the emotional poverty she believed to be her pathetic lot, acquires a wealth of experience and insight and rediscovers her own prince. As she looks forward to making her life with Rodney in their own place and to her genuine involvement at St. Luke's, she concludes that her life is "a glass of blessings." In George Herbert's poem, God creates man with many wonderful attributes but withholds rest, so that "If goodnesse leade him not, yet wearinesse / May tosse him to my breast." Wilmet, rich in many ways, is tossed into a measure of devoutness by her restlessness—and by Piers's sexual preference.

Dulcie Mainwaring is closely related to Mildred Lathbury (*EW*): the great question for her as the heroine of *No Fond Return of Love* is whether to observe or participate in life. However, the issue seems academic because Dulcie is so isolated, lacking even the little Church-centered community that is the social foundation of Mildred's life. Like Mildred, she has lost her parents, and she is not particularly close to her married sister. Mildred's part-time work for the distressed gentlewomen and her church activities put her in touch with others, but Dulcie's work as an indexer and proofreader is a solitary job done at home. Curiously, she considers her occupation "degrading." Her work, as she sees it, is a touchstone for her life: "more brilliant" people write the manuscripts, she does the secondary mechanical tasks with which they cannot be bothered. She seems to accept as her lot a humdrum, undistinguished existence.

Dulcie thinks her life is at a critical point because, almost a year ago, Maurice Clive broke their engagement on the grounds that she was too good for him. (This young man agrees, apparently, that the good are often boring.) From her experience of love and subsequent misery, the pain blocks all memory of happy affection; consequently, she has almost decided that it is safer "to observe [others'] joys and sorrows with detachment as if one were watching a film or a play." Though what she sees often upsets her, Dulcie still employs her talents as a researcher, learning what she can about particular people from public records and, where possible, from on-site visits (once under an assumed name, invented on the spot). Though she says that after "one great sorrow, or one great love" "we only want the trivial things," the subjects of her "research into the lives of ordinary people" are both attractive men—Aylwin Forbes and his brother Neville. Moreover, she fights her own unacknowledged loneliness by befriending the reluctant and prickly Viola Dace.

While Dulcie sits on the banks of Lake Observation, her toes dangling in its tranquil water, Senhor MacBride-Pereira floats (decorously, and with eyes wide open) midlake. The half-life of emotional retirement might seem to be a more viable option for women, whose proper sphere was assumed for so long to be of the hemi-variety, but Pym reminds us that the attitude is not sexually determined. A courtly Anglophile given to jotting down British colloquialisms, Senhor MacBride-Pereira has two secret delights: wearing a kilt in the MacBride plaid and watching people from the time-honored upstairs window. Just as we might eat Jujie fruits or popcorn at the movies, he munches grilled or sugared almonds as he watches Paul and Laurel, Viola and Bill Sedge, or Aylwin coming and going to Dulcie's house. The Brazilian makes life at the window look pleasant, but then he is a diplomat in his late fifties and not a woman in her early thirties. Our heroine's passionate nosiness may match and even surpass Senhor MacBride-Pereira's, but she has not retired to the window to watch the dumb show.

A secret kilt-wearer is obviously a person of some imagination, and we can easily guess at the identity the Senhor creates for himself by baring his knees. To some extent, many of us are Walter or Wanda Mittys, but some of us do not require human props, as does Aylwin Forbes, a male counterpart of Prudence Bates (*JP*). At forty-seven, Aylwin is "beautiful" enough to make Viola and then Dulcie pause in their indexing. He is as self-conscious in his beauty as Prudence or Wilmet Forsyth, though his exaggerated sense of dignity is his own. Just as Prudence, lovely and self-dramatizing, imagined herself in strangers' eyes as a compelling figure of muted sorrow, so Aylwin, playing to an unseen audience, fears he might look ridiculous carrying a large bunch of flowers. This gentleman scholar and editor of a literary journal, resourceful enough to find a "neo-metaphysical" poet "so obscure that not even the Americans had 'done' him," has an imagined self, a hackneyed role that shapes his life. He is, he believes, "an impetuous romantic" whose nature dictates unsuitable choices in women.

It is a bit inaccurate to speak of Aylwin's *creation* of a self because his father preceded him in the role, as if romantic impetuosity were a genetically transmitted trait. But several of Pym's characters either deliberately fashion the identities they show others or at least see the possibility of another self. Laurel comes to London as the country girl and transforms herself eventually into the city sophisticate. Violet has become "Viola," discarding any flowery sweetness of manner or appearance for brusqueness and an untidy rakishness. Aylwin, who exposes her unkindly as the "violet by the mossy stone" to Dulcie and Maurice, knows she presents a particular self to him and avoids her especially on one occasion when she is sporting red-canvas shoes. Though he is often eager to avoid her, there is a touch of sensitivity in his decision not to surprise her in a non-Viola guise. Subsequently, when Bill Sedge remarks on meeting her that "a shade of blue, almost *violet*" is her color, Viola is charmed by the stranger who discovers her inmost self, astounded into acknowledging the hitherto rejected name.

In addition to seeing herself as one who does the boring and inglorious tasks for others, Dulcie sees herself as the sort of nice person someone like Viola might use. She is flattered to be used. She flirts with a tragic role, the woman with the great love and great sorrow, but without conviction because she is too sensible. (This is just as well, really, because somehow the part does not seem right for a woman with thin legs and thick shoes.) Because she is not certain what kind of life she wants, she has no clearly defined sense of self, except as she imagines others' images of her. She guesses rightly, for instance, that Viola sees her as "rather dreary but a good-natured soul."

Still, when Dulcie recognizes her double, a potential self, at the Bond Street gallery where Maurice works, her feelings are mixed:

> The young woman seemed a more elegant version of herself, rather as Dulcie might have looked if some woman's magazine has taken her in hand. The fair hair was elegantly folded into a kind of pleat at the back of the head, the eyes shadowed with blue, and the finger-nails painted with a pearly pink varnish. Dulcie turned away and sighed. It was a little upsetting to see what one might have been. (89)

She is a bit distressed, but accepts the difference between her plain self and its gussied-up version. Unlike Mildred Lathbury, Dulcie exerts no effort to make *more* of herself, even when Miss Lord, her housekeeper, takes it upon herself to give counsel in the art. The novel includes a career woman, Jessica Foy, who has made a successful and happy life, but Dulcie (like her beauty counselor) considers marriage the be-all and end-all; therefore, "a man's got to notice you, hasn't he—that's the first step," so Dulcie, according to Miss Lord, needs "Head bigger ['the bouffant style'] and eyes bigger." In private, she fluffs up her hair and decides her eyes *are* small, but that is the extent of her attention to deliberate self-creation.

In the creation of selves, people usually work from an image that appeals to them, however odious or ludicrous it might seem to others; but in the creation of others, people can make everything from stick figures to monsters to unblemished dolls. In this novel, as in *Jane and Prudence*, Pym stresses the fashioning of others with which people are unconsciously and endlessly busy. Some of these images are static, but others are modified because the makers' own feelings change or because people "don't always act in character," not the character given them by others or even the character they have themselves chosen. Aylwin, for example, usually sees Viola as an unattractive, pursuing woman, but at one point as a pathetic figure so unhinged by passion for him that she wears those red-canvas shoes. In addition to achieving complexity of characterization, the author makes wonderful comedy from her characters' limited perspectives and from the simple strategies they adopt to deal with multifaceted individuals. Viola, looking at Aylwin, sees an utterly desirable, suffering man who should turn to her for consolation after Marjorie leaves. But Aylwin is not suffering and refuses to turn to Viola in spite of the many opportunities she gives him.

Marjorie Williton Forbes sees her estranged husband as a vaguely fearsome but unlikable and boring man. She briefly envisions him, in their separation, as a potentially romantic figure, the man who might storm the old dragon's chintzy den to reclaim his love-treasure. But Aylwin fails as her hero. A jumble sale, attended by women like Rhoda Wellcome (*LTA*) chatting about Deirdre and Digby Fox and their expected baby, is the challenge the knight cannot meet, and Marjorie's first "Aylwin" stands. The old dragon, Mrs. Williton, invests her son-in-law with glamour by seeing him as "a libertine," the creaky word suggesting all sorts of deliciously scandalous behavior. She expects Aylwin to be morally outrageous, so everything titillates the straitlaced woman, even his vacation in Tuscany. The "Aylwin" seen by his mother and Neville, his clergyman brother, is clever and handsome but foolish, devoid of sense about women. He is essentially harmless in their view, but still a worry to them. Mrs. Forbes's concern is mingled with indulgent pride because she favors him as a version of her long-dead husband.

Dulcie starts recreating Aylwin from the moment he faints at the scholarly conference and she observes that "he's beautiful . . . like a Greek marble . . . the features a little blunted, with the charm of being not quite perfect." Her attraction to him turns him into a hero, a central figure whose existence, she believes, defines the lives of women: Marjorie, the wife who returns to her mother; Viola, the acknowledged and disappointed admirer; and Dulcie herself, the secret admirer resigned to loving from a discreet distance. She makes her Aylwin extraordinary: for "Mothering Sunday," he sends Mrs. Forbes not a mundane card, Dulcie guesses, but a piece of antique jewelry or a case of wine. After meeting Marjorie, she sees him as a man who married "beneath" himself, and she eventually finds a comfortable explanation. Visiting the Forbes castle in Taviscombe with Viola, Dulcie notices a tall woman whose elegance makes her feel her own relative shabbiness. Wilmet Forsyth (*GB*), "cherished and secure with her three men," Keith, Piers, and Rodney, repeats the local story of the unsuitable marriage of Aylwin's parents. Initially, Dulcie accepts the hereditary theory for Aylwin's choice of Marjorie, a theory with the virtues of being romantic and implying no fault on his part. When she hears that he has sent Laurel a postcard, she turns him into an avuncular figure concerned about her niece's "cultural education"; but this sweet invention falls to pieces when she is forced to see him as an "old man" who might propose, very improperly, to Laurel. Though he seems, as a man who "always" wants unsuitable wives, almost contemptible to her, her infatuation insists that he is "a rare person." Finally, after Marjorie's elopement and Laurel's refusal, she sees him as the embodiment of a fantasy, the lonely man who might turn to her, by default, for consolation, the man who represents all her hope for an emotional life.

Our own response to Aylwin, especially as he courts Laurel, is bound to be more complex and less sympathetic than Dulcie's. Pym does not tell us much about his marriage, but once Marjorie is gone, he makes no serious effort to set his marriage to rights. His vanity is laughable when he refuses to enter Dulcie's house with Maurice, a good-looking man younger than he, but irritating when he cannot understand the gap between a girl's nineteen years and his own forty-seven or forty-eight. He assumes, despite Dulcie's blunt talk, that Laurel will have him, and is not deterred by the impropriety of offering himself while still married. Typically, he is patronizing and petty about women, thinking, for instance, that they smoke more than men "because of the emptiness of their lives, no doubt, most of them being unmarried."

Pym presents Dulcie to us in the same kaleidoscope style that reveals Aylwin, conveying again the sense that no one sees or addresses the whole, complex person. Miss Lord works for a deserving young woman who keeps men at a distance by reading too much (the consequence of her impractical literary education) and by being needlessly drab. The good woman is stung by the messy Viola's engagement while the tidy Dulcie languishes in unappreciation. Laurel deals with an aunt who is past it, an ancient relative well beyond any romantic feelings, whose "dull and lonely" life might make her cling to a niece who wants independence. Viola, though close to Dulcie's age, regards her as an interfering "do-gooder," "Already half way to being a dim English spinster." Disarmed by Dulcie's good-natured openness, Viola comes to see her more positively, as a confidante, though she can never fully understand her friend's eccentric researches into others' lives and her deflating, commonsensical approach. During a trying moment, for example, when Viola wonders what would happen if the tears of injured merit ran down her cheeks, she realizes that Dulcie would be the only one who noticed—but that she would probably suggest some cold remedy.

Maurice Clive, the handsome man who claimed, in a way, to be too bad to marry Dulcie, sees her as "good, 'like bread,'" a woman "as vulnerable and unsophisticated as a girl of eighteen." Evidently her goodness does not spoil or stale, and she appeals to him anew after nearly a year apart. But Dulcie knows this man cannot live on bread alone and discourages him, so he finally approaches her as "somebody to tell [his] troubles to," the perfect confidante. Aylwin's first "Miss Mainwaring" is a stable, respectable figure, a friend who might steady Viola. Observing Maurice's relative intimacy with her and determined not to be outdone, he progresses to "Dulcie." However, as his infatuation with Laurel develops, she becomes "Miss Mainwaring—Laurel's aunt," as if she had become as decrepit to him as she seems to her niece. He speaks to her in this guise, depressing Dulcie, about his hopes for the future with her niece. And she changes immediately, as if his remarks had been a sorcerer's formula. The old aunt becomes interesting by her transformation into an indignant, blunt, and even intimidating woman:

> What a surprising conversation with that nice Miss Mainwaring—Dulcie—he thought. Perhaps there were hidden depths there. He realized that he was almost afraid of her and glanced back quickly over his shoulder to see if she were following. (224)

Hidden depths are more appropriate to strudel than to bread, and Aylwin's "Dulcie," by the time he recreates her (and himself), is infinitely more appealing than Maurice's blandly edible fiancée: she is Jane Austen's Fanny Price to his Edmund Bertram.

As was the case with Aylwin, the various characters' perspectives on Dulcie do not add up to the woman revealed to the reader. Our Dulcie is more tenderhearted than Viola realizes, fretting over the troubles of unknown beggars and African students, but also less good than Maurice believes. She has a sly sense of humor and a loopy slant of the imagination that leads her to wonder, for example, if anonymous phone calls are made by people like her with "an odd ten minutes to fill in before arriving somewhere." To herself, she scorns Marjorie's style and tastes. When her friend is happy to be courted by Bill Sedge, Dulcie is disappointed in her: "Viola was just a rather dull woman, wanting only to be loved." Just as she cannot admit her own loneliness when she persuades herself at first that Viola needs her friendship, she cannot admit that she too wants "only" to be loved, however dull and unoriginal such a desire might make her. Surely, good-as-bread people do not pry into the affairs of others, at least not with the method and dedication Dulcie brings to her hobby. Obviously, Maurice did not care enough to discover that she has a few redeeming faults.

Maurice is not the only one to give another no fond return of love. Fairly early in the novel, Dulcie sees an image of unrequited love that returns to trouble her: Miss Spicer runs through the church weeping after Neville rejects her proffered love. In spite of seeing the pain of this unknown woman, and in spite of her own experience with Maurice, Dulcie at first glorifies the idea of endless, unrequited love, along with Viola:

> "There are some people one could never cease to care for," said Viola, "and I suppose Aylwin is one of those."
> "Obviously every man must be that to some woman," said Dulcie, "even the most unworthy man." She had been thinking of Maurice, but surely she had ceased to "care" for him? "Of course," she went on, "those are the people from whom one asks no return of love, if you see what I mean. Just to be allowed to love them is enough." (75)

If the women were correct, practically all of the characters would be satisfied people because most experience unrequited love, and some for "unworthy" objects. There is no fond return of love from Neville to Miss Spicer, from Maurice to Dulcie, from Aylwin to Viola, from Aylwin to Dulcie (until the last minute), or from Laurel to Aylwin.

The novel gives so much emphasis to suitability in romantic choices and to Aylwin's penchant for inappropriate women that it invites us to classify all its unrequited or requited loves as suitable or unsuitable. Aylwin's love for Marjorie, sometime in the past, was clearly unsuitable on the grounds of education and interests. His awareness that his father had made an unsuitable choice (according to social class) but a happy marriage might have encouraged him; but the novel suggests that it is not until after Marjorie leaves him, especially when he has decided on divorce, that he fully realizes she was "totally unsuitable." But by then, "here he was being true to form [as 'an impetuous romantic'], thinking of marrying a girl half his age!" The fact that Laurel is unsuitable because of her age and inexperience as well as her education and interests does not bother him at all. It is, the silly man thinks, his destiny to love unwisely. Ironically, Dulcie, who so confidently scolds Aylwin for his folly, has significant things in common with him. Her choice of Maurice was entirely unsuitable, and she judges that theirs would have been an awful marriage "with the wife a little older and a little taller and a great deal more intelligent than the husband"—but, like Aylwin, she discovers the total unsuitability only in retrospect.

Viola's love for Aylwin was marvelously suitable. But her being of the right age and sharing his scholarly interests failed to ignite romance; in fact, her suitability aroused his insecure fears about mature women:

> he had known from the beginning that Marjorie could never enter into his work with him, but he had been touched and flattered by her show of interest . . . And the way she had looked—so fragile and appealing with her fluffy curls, almost a "girl wife"—had been such a refreshing change from the frightening elegance, frowsty bohemianism, or uncompromising dowdiness, of those women who could really have entered into his work and would probably in the end have elbowed him out of it altogether. (81)

Viola, watching him drool over the dewy-fresh Laurel, understands in a flash his choice of Marjorie and is disenchanted but, perhaps because she is so "embarrassed and disgusted," does not share her insight with Dulcie. For the same reasons that Viola's love for Aylwin is suitable, Dulcie's is too. But while Laurel is willing to be his girl-love, he is not at all attracted to her uncompromisingly plain aunt.

The forthcoming marriage of Viola to Bill Sedge at first seems unsuitable to Dulcie because of the couple's different backgrounds and interests. When she hears Hermione locate the unsuitability in the vague regions of class, Bill being an immigrant and her cook's brother, Dulcie understands what she means. But she defends her friend's choice: "Love isn't always suitable," she tells the old woman who has just made an eminently appropriate match.

Dulcie finds the thought of her aunt's suitable forthcoming marriage "at once satisfactory and depressing." She has intuited, at last, that love is the alchemy transmuting suitable and unsuitable materials alike into the shiny, treasured prize. When she calls Aylwin "a rare person," Perspective, borrowing the thunderous voice of Miss Randall, answers, "A rather good-looking man who has made a mess of his marriage, by all accounts—I shouldn't have thought that was rare at all." A short while later, thanks to Viola's "short dark gentleman," the lightning flashes for Dulcie: "When one loved somebody, everything about him—imperfections, vices even—became rare and special." She had been partly right earlier, when she remarked that some men "don't really want what's good for them"; men and women want what they love, period. And lovers have brains nimble in the discovery of the good or the suitability that eludes others, though not always capable of unwavering adherence to that discovery.

Despite Dulcie's awareness, she seems at the end to have come full circle, back to the lonely spot where she started. Laurel and Viola are gone, and Aylwin is presumably lost to some new girl willing to console him. Such a fate hardly seems fair to a woman who chose participation and risked rejection by offering herself to Aylwin under the guise of "somebody who can appreciate your work and help you with it." When her unquenchable curiosity sends her back to Neville's church, he seems to offer her the role vacated by Miss Spicer. Because Dulcie can envision herself falling in love with him and running tearfully through the church, she will not settle for another unrequited love. Loving Aylwin without hope has been painful enough to dispel her notion that "just to be allowed to love [some people] is enough."

Aylwin's call is at least a reprieve for her from a life of observation, though he hopes to change her situation entirely. Indeed, he has already changed Dulcie entirely. The best he could think about her, when he was infatuated with Laurel, was that it was *just* possible to imagine she might once have had the "exciting freshness" so evident in her niece. Since mature women threaten him, he was bound to notice then that "she still had that trusting, vulnerable look in her eyes" that usually goes with inexperience. Her outspoken outburst suggested to him, we remember, that she might have "hidden depths." But after Marjorie has eloped and Laurel has rejected him, the full power of creative imagination shows itself. Some are born glamorous, some achieve glamour, but Dulcie has glamour thrust upon her: she is Fanny Price, a literary heroine. Even more dazzling is Aylwin's bestowal of unsuitability on his new love:

> Yet here he was being true to type after all. For what might seem to the rest of the world an eminently "suitable" marriage to a woman no longer very young, who could help him with his work, now seemed to him the most unsuitable that could be imagined, simply because it had never occurred to him that he could love such a person. It was all most delightfully incongruous. Just the sort of thing Aylwin Forbes would do. (253)

We have remarked previously on the wonders of the human mind. But what of Dulcie? She is willing to greet him and be gathered to his heart. She decides instantaneously that it will be "more satisfying" to work for him than to become Miss Spicer, and it occurs to her that maybe, "in his loneliness," he is turning to her. Whichever way, he is just right for her: if she wants a suitable lover, she can think of their relative ages and their common interests; if, on the other hand, she wants an unsuitable attachment, she can focus on his upcoming divorce and his courtship of her niece—which would certainly make for interesting family reunions.

Dulcie may have been too good for Maurice, but Aylwin cannot be too bad for Dulcie. She knows him—the worst about him—but she wants him. Only a very powerful sexual attraction can account for her readiness to accept him, as only humiliation and the fear of being alone can account for Aylwin's about-face and eagerness to "love" her. What with Marjorie, Viola, and Laurel, Aylwin has never been, in the course of the novel, without the attention of a woman. This conclusion is, like Aunt Hermione's engagement, "at once satisfactory and depressing." The fact that Aylwin sees Dulcie (and himself) as a fictional character suggests that the woman he expects to find is unreal—a figment of his imagination rather than the "real" Dulcie he knows so slightly, a fact which does not seem promising for their future together. But when we remember the "Dulcie" in the minds of other characters, we have to ask whether Viola's interfering do-gooder or Laurel's dried-up old relative are better as reflections of the "real" woman—or more likely to assist her in the attainment of her desires. Pym emphasizes the unreality on which romantic love is based, but she also insists that the imaginative re-creation of others is not undertaken only by lovers.

Inviting Aylwin to tea, Dulcie accepts participation; risking pain in the hope of fulfillment, she saves her own emotional life. Since she does not know yet that she is a heroine, her hope springs from the beggarly attitude that she might console him for the loss of another. There is no thought, on her part, of meeting him as an equal, as a woman desirable in herself. Just as she believes she is useful as an indexer to people more brilliant than herself, she hopes to be useful as a nurse for the hurt inflicted by women more attractive to him than herself.

As we saw, all the major characters in the novel are engaged in the re-creation of others, but Dulcie's realization that "she had created [Viola] and that she had not come up to expectations, like a character in a book who had failed to come alive," together with her commitment to observation, makes her unique. Late in the novel, she has misgivings when she realizes that her snooping is a form of aggression in which her subjects become "victims," and even thinks her observation might *cause* things to happen. In this, she is wrong. In direct contrast to this amateur voyeur, Pym introduces herself, as Dulcie and Viola's fellow guest at the Anchorage, the hotel that advertises a "bright Christian atmosphere":

> She was a woman of about forty, ordinary-looking and unaccompanied [so] nobody took much notice of her. As it happened, she was a novelist; indeed, some of the occupants of the tables had read and enjoyed her books, but it would never have occurred to them to connect her name, even had they ascertained it from the hotel register, with that of the author they admired. They ate their stewed plums and custard and drank their thimble-sized cups of coffee, quite unconscious that they were being observed. (176)

Dulcie's bathroom library includes *Some Tame Gazelle*, and

she believes novelists (and private detectives) have a purpose and therefore an excuse for their interest in others' lives and behavior: content as she is to be used by others, perhaps she would have been flattered to be captured, with Viola, as something like "two women on the brink of spinsterhood—fair one with thin legs almost resigned, sallow one with bizarre makeup still trying—dining together at Christian hotel."

Pym shared, as we know from *A Very Private Eye*, Dulcie's "passion for 'finding out' about people who interested or attracted her," the hobby of "research into the lives of ordinary people"; but her diaries are full of strangers and scenes that, having caught her eye, were stored for possible use, like the elderly waitress with a "little wrinkled claw-like hand" or the "two nuns buying a typewriter in Selfridges. Oh, what were they going to do with it?" There are differences as well as similarities, her appearance here suggests, between the curiosity and creativity of the amateur observer and the novelist. Dulcie observes strangers and sometimes creates little scenarios around them, such as her fantasy of the beggar sitting comfortably before his television at home, no longer hugging himself to mime pain. But her imagination does not have the power or the discipline to make a man with the detailed and unique history that would lead him at some point to beg wrongfully, under false dolors, as it were. Moreover, Dulcie is not inclined to expend real energy on strangers.

Giving her heroine her own inquisitive hobby and hinting that she once saw the actual prototypes for "Dulcie" and "Viola," the author suggests that Pym the research hobbyist and Pym the novelist are not identical, though both have their being from the same curiosity. The researcher cannot cause things to happen to those she observes, but the novelist can, and in *No Fond Return of Love* Pym is a generous creator who gives some of her women the fulfillment of their romantic fantasies. Marjorie gets her ridiculous wish to meet a romantic stranger on the train. The dream that the wished-for man will turn, finally, for consolation to the obvious and deserving lady comes true for Hermione. We can assume she has coveted, for ages, the woman's place in the vicarage.

Realization of the same fantasy is imminent for Dulcie because she expressed her indignation about Aylwin's desire to marry Laurel:

> She was by no means at her best this morning, though if it had been a romantic novel, she thought, he would have been struck by how handsome she looked when she was angry, the sea breeze having whipped some colour into her normally pale cheeks. (223)

In the unfailing combination of the sea breeze and her anger, Aylwin glimpses the "hidden depths" that he hopes to explore if his fantasy of claiming his unsuitable Fanny is granted.

An Unsuitable Attachment

At a dinner party attended by Everard Bone (*EW*) and Gervase Fairfax (*LTA*), the talk turns to the similarity between novelists, who write the same book many times over, and anthropologists, who rehash the same material in many books and articles: "both study life in communities, though the novelist need not be so accurate or bother with statistics and kinship tables." Ianthe Broome protests about the repetitive novelist that "life can be interpreted in so many ways" and adds that he has the advantage over the anthropologist since "he can let his imagination go where it will." In *An Unsuitable Attachment*, only a very minor character is a novelist, but people are continually "studying" each other and letting their imaginations run wild. The distortions attending observation create much of the novel's humor, the expectations people have of each other most of its complications, but as its title indicates, the plot particularly centers on unsuitable attachments. In the context of Pym's broadening vision, the book is especially interesting in its portrayal of Rupert Stonebird, one of the author's most interesting and sympathetic men.

When Daisy Pettigrew puts on her glasses to get a good view of the vicarage garden next door, she spies a statue, probably, she thinks, of the Virgin Mary. Daisy watches Sophia Ainger, the vicar's wife, come outside and start to make some obeisance; instead, she destroys the "popish image"—by removing a blue cloth that had been drying on a tree stump. Looking, as she passes by, into the windows of Rupert's house, Penelope Grandison sees him and an indistinct woman, standing by a table holding a loaf of bread, cheese, and two glasses. Her chagrin at "the Omar Khayyam-like details" increases when she hears Rupert at his door, calling goodbye to "Esther," "some glamorous Jewess, no doubt." But she almost kisses the fiftyish woman who overtakes her, asking directions to the bus. Esther Clovis (*EW* and *LTA*), she judges, cannot possibly be a rival for Rupert's affections. These people are continually observing each other and doing a laughable job of interpreting what they see or think they see. They believe they see and interpret truly, but unknowingly they are as imaginative as writers of fiction. By these and other such instances, Pym suggests how difficult it is for one person to know another or understand what he does, thinks, or feels.

Though these people are unconsciously creative as they watch each other, they think and judge in terms of stereotypes, expecting those around them to conform to these inflexible patterns. Ianthe, for instance, is a woman who practices Christian charity. Loving one's neighbor is a duty she understands as doing good to somebody for whom one feels no particular affection. So she trots off to visit Miss Grimes, the woman who has recently retired as her coworker in the library, expecting to bring Christmas cheer to a destitute and lonely old lady. Alas, she finds Miss Grimes living almost graciously. She is surrounded by "some rather good pieces of furniture and china" and offers as refreshment a glass of fairly good wine. Ianthe is upset that the woman is not more needy, and resentful that she takes the violets and Madeira meant for herself. For the same kind of reason, Ianthe disapproves of Sophia. A vicar's wife should not express her dissatisfaction, saying she and her husband are not as close as she would like. By the time Sophia laments that we all have to do "dull unnecessary things" rather than enjoyable ones, Ianthe's attitude toward her is set. She hears "dull necessary things" and is primly disapproving—a vicar's wife is not supposed to say such things.

Ianthe is not the only one who has preconceptions, expectations based on them, and subsequent little shocks of discovery. One of the loveliest images in the novel is the little bundle of lemon leaves that must be unwrapped, leaf by leaf, "to reach the deliciously flavoured raisins at the heart." As Sophia realizes, the fragrant bundle has "something in common with uncovering the secrets of the heart." But she does not see the suggestion of vulnerability in the image or understand that she does not even come close to the raisins in her dealings with people. Her expectations, like those of the other characters, center especially on Rupert and Ianthe as the newcomers to her husband's parish. Rupert, on first sight, seems a prospective husband for her sister Penelope. However, like any matchmaker confronted with a candidate who seems too good to be true, she assumes that this good-looking man in his mid-thirties must be ineligible. One by one, to her delight, her expectations of his unsuitability are dispelled.

Penelope, just recovering from one of her frequent romantic disappointments, is not inhibited by any idea of male worthiness. Men and women, she tells her married sister, never match each other in being "good enough"—life is imperfect, and Penny, at twenty-five, wants a husband. Attracted to a handsome, eligible man, she assumes as a matter of course that he has women friends and is pursued by them (and by Ianthe). When he goes to visit "friends in the country," she imagines him surrounded by beautiful women. She expects to attract him by wearing elegant or trendy things, by devising strategies on her own and with Sophia, and by flirting with him. If he is interested, she expects that he will flirt back, pursue her with invitations to good places, and give physical signs of his interest. In short, she expects Rupert to be a typical man, aware of his own value as an eligible bachelor, and practiced in the standard moves of the romantic game.

Penelope's expectations, and her sister's, cannot be met because Rupert is not the man they imagine. Though he has begun to think he wants to marry, he has no circle of women friends from which to consider possibilities. Far from spending a glamorous holiday in the country, he has a quiet visit with a married couple and their small children. When he is not at the infrequent social function in some way connected with the people he has met at St. Basil's, he spends most of his time working at home or at the Foresight Research Center, surrounded by people like Everard Bone, Apfelbaum (*EW*), Fairfax, Felix Mainwaring, and Esther Clovis (*LTA*), and occasionally chatting about work done by people like Digby Fox. A man who spends most of his time correcting proofs, reading scholarly articles, or marking students' papers, he is not the swinging bachelor who eludes women clamoring to be Mrs. Stonebird.

If Barbara Pym wrote about "excellent men," Rupert might be one of them: in his air of inexperience and awkwardness with the opposite sex, as in his essential decency, he resembles women like Mildred Lathbury Bone. A man who sees a woman looking unattractively ill, decides she is "obviously in need of cherishing," and fills her hot-water bottle while she shuffles back to bed is obviously a gem, however rough his exterior. But he is wretched at making passable conversation or smoothing over those little awkward situations that from time to time daunt the best of us. His recovery of faith he takes seriously, and conscience makes him sensitive to the mysterious hurts he thinks he might have inflicted on Penelope. He often tries to be an observer, even dressing unobtrusively in order not to draw attention to himself, not because he wants to be detached, but because he is shy. He does not assume that women will be interested in his work, and hardly talks about it for fear of boring them. Modest, he cannot imagine that Penelope is seriously interested in him. Unfortunately, every time he tries to take a positive step toward her, he is thwarted by circumstances. Comically klutzy and hugely worried even about extending a simple invitation to an anthropologists' garden party, he never quite manages to deliver the kisses he intends. Just as Dulcie sometimes feels like a "woman manquée," or Mildred inept because she does not know how to color and costume herself, Rupert worries that he will not appear manly if he does not talk knowingly about wine or if he cannot make a taxi materialize at the right moment. A bird longing to fly into romance and marriage, he seems grounded by wings of stone.

Rupert is interested in both Penelope and Ianthe and does not realize that his indecision springs from a deep conventionality. The first time he sees the women, he labels Ianthe as "pretty but uninteresting" and Penelope as the "Pre-

Raphaelite beatnik." Certainly, the last description sounds more compelling, but Rupert is not persuaded that a woman who seems offbeat to his fairly innocent eyes is for him. He is not given, either, to analyzing or understanding his feelings. Therefore, since he is an archdeacon's son, Ianthe has the advantage by being a canon's daughter. He has not known her too long before the absolute correctness of her appearance makes him think "not that he loved her but that he would like to see her always in his house, like some suitable decoration or finishing touch." She wears blue wool to his dinner party, while Penelope, determined to make a contrast, is ablaze in silver lamé, too short and too tight. Believing that both women admire him, he feels a sense of power, which is quickly deflated by the realization that, with both women present, he can do nothing. However, when he notices that Penny's dress is split in the back, he decides to give her a goodnight kiss—a plan foiled by Sophia's presence on the doorstep of the vicarage.

In Rome, the pattern repeats itself. Seeing Ianthe's proper little tourist costume, he finds her "rather more than just suitable"; but noticing Penny's "dusty little toes" in her sandals, Rupert finds her attractive also, in an "outlandish" way. A combination of too much wine, the realization that he would rather be alone with Ianthe, and his social ineptitude makes Penny cry by the Spanish Steps, whereupon the mystified Rupert wants to kiss her and go to bed with her. But by the time he leads her to a more secluded spot (the conventional locale for a kiss), Penny has recovered. Mortified and deeply wounded by his calling her "a jolly little thing," she composes herself. The moment for the kiss passes. He is thwarted again when he wants to make amends to her (for whatever it was that made her cry) by taking her to the garden party at the research center. She says she cannot go during a painfully stupid telephone conversation, in which Rupert cannot get out the words to invite her to dinner. So he takes Ianthe. For the first time, seeing her in her garden-party clothes, he realizes that she reminds him of his mother at similar parish functions and wonders, "Was this quite as it should be?" But he lacks the sense to explore this, and tries, after the party, to kiss Ianthe. She bursts into tears. Understandably, Rupert is astonished that he, "the meekest and kindest of men," has made another woman cry.

Ianthe is visibly a gentlewoman, the sort of old-fashioned lady who expects courtesy from men, as Pym remarks, and sometimes gets it. The other characters see her at thirty-five as a woman devoted to convention, propriety, the Church, and good works. We have already mentioned her Christian charity to Miss Grimes, an act originating in genuine conviction—even if she feels an uncharitable disappointment at the relative prosperity of the neighbor she chooses to succor. She is shy with men, involved in her church circle, and a good cook and housekeeper. Like other Pym women, Ianthe has "good" family things and enjoys financial security, even owning her house. Unfortunately, she is a bit of a prude, and we can easily understand why some of her acquaintances think she is "too good to be true." She is inhibited and very class-conscious; she would not dream of making herself a drink at home after work or even of having a cup of tea like the "working classes"; and she attaches a tremendous importance to propriety, knowing automatically what is right or wrong for her. She lacks, also, the humor, imagination, and openness of most of Pym's heroines. She is not amused by jokes about hymns, not much interested in other people, and critical of those whom she does not understand.

Naturally, other people have expectations of her. Mark imagines that, since she is of the right class, she will be a good friend of Sophia's, but Ianthe never warms to the vicar's wife. Rupert expects the proper Miss Broome to welcome his proper attentions, but she thinks of him as "a brother" or, more often, simply as a near-neighbor. Mark and Sophia have her pegged as an excellent woman, who of course does not marry. Even Penny, who expects Ianthe as a single woman to be her dark horse rival for Rupert, cannot see her as a person with feelings. It is hard, she tells Ianthe, to envision her falling in love with anyone: "You're so cool and collected and I'm sure a man would have to be almost perfect to come up to your standards." Of all Pym's women, Ianthe does seem least likely to desire or find romance—she is not nearly as charming, interesting, or amusing as Mildred Lathbury, Catherine Oliphant, or Dulcie Mainwaring. For pure appeal, she does not have a prayer against Belinda Bede.

Yet, though people do not change their opinions of her, she starts surprising them almost immediately. Excellent women do not have good-looking male friends, thinks Sophia, when Mervyn Cantrell and John Challow, Ianthe's coworkers at the library, come to see her at the St. Basil's church bazaar. Penelope, who worries that older women of twenty-five do not attract men like girls of eighteen, is surprised to see a handsome man in Rome staring at Ianthe. It develops, unromantically enough, that Basil Branche, now traveling with the Misses Bede (one of whom inherited the property of an Italian count who always hoped to marry her), was a curate of Ianthe's father. But, on an evening when Penny herself is out with a girlfriend, she runs into Ianthe dining out with Mervyn. It is a great surprise to everyone that this rigid stick of a Miss Broome has three suitors. Mervyn, the head librarian, whose absorbing mother must sometime die, like Wilf Bason's (*GB*), is suitable and covets Ianthe's fine things, especially her Pembroke table and Hepplewhite chairs. He has the decency at least not to feign love and to base his proposal on a reasonable practicality. Rupert, whose claim to Ianthe, if he could ever manage to claim anything, might be made on grounds of pure suitability, we have already mentioned. But Ianthe cries when he is about to kiss her because she, whose sure foundation is conventional propriety, is in love with the totally unsuitable John Challow. As she sees it herself, John is all wrong because of his class and education. Besides, this man, who wears shoes unlike any worn by people of Ianthe's own kind, is thirty to her thirty-five.

What separates John and Ianthe is her own rigidity, a barrier she must shatter in order to accept her own feelings. When John comes to work at the library, he is attracted by her "air of good breeding" from the beginning. She knows what his disturbing glances mean, but avoids him and tries to stay coolly aloof. Still, John touches her. The first time it happens, she realizes that he actually *needs* his paycheck, and seeing his post office savings-book, she is moved more profoundly than she could ever be by ardent glances. Again, she is flattered that he has followed her into her uncle's church for a noontime service, but his thin coat on a cold day registers, as even the most gratifying flattery cannot do, on her heart. The last stroke comes when John is sick, absent from work, and Ianthe, fully conscious that her mother would disapprove of it as "most unsuitable," goes to visit. She tries to persuade herself that she can enter the visit in her moral ledger under "Charity and Good Works," right beneath her call on Miss Grimes, "visiting the sick" being an unquestionable Christian duty. Arriving with her gifts of daffodils and lemon barley water, she is appalled at the meanness of his room. She washes dishes and tidies up his tatty bed-sitter, silently but deeply indignant that he, who "loved beautiful things, she felt sure," should have to live as he does. She regrets the stern conventions that forbid her taking him, as a lodger, into her own roomy house. She even lends him money, "glad that he felt able to ask her."

Shortly thereafter, when John kisses her at the train station, Ianthe is forced to acknowledge that she has changed:

> That John should have kissed her like that—in the way she had quite often seen boys kiss girls on their way home—and that she should not have minded, apart from the slight awkwardness of the people surging around them, would have seemed incredible to her a few months ago. One did not behave like that in a public place with a young man, suitable or otherwise, and John was so very much otherwise. (137)

As with Rupert's sporadic tenderness for Penelope (which he ignores), Ianthe is won by John's vulnerability, by the "pity which is akin to love." These are feelings toward a particular someone shared by no one else. Neither Ianthe nor Sophia, for instance, notice Penny's "dusty little toes," feel that her split dress makes her "endearing," or think that she has "something slightly comic about her appearance." Rupert notices these things because the "Pre-Raphaelite beatnik" appeals to him with a pathos he alone perceives. It is the same with Ianthe and John. Mervyn Cantrell does not see a vulnerable, touching young man. His knowledge that John is not well off does not wring his librarian heart; it makes him see an unscrupulous gold-digger who wants to latch on to a good thing in a naive woman and her comfortable situation. He almost dispels Ianthe's vision of the fragrant raisins hidden in the lemony bundle, but she deliberately accepted her love for John in Rome, and accepts his as soon as he declares himself.

When Sophia learns of Ianthe's interest in a man, she cruelly tries to make her friend conform to her expectations, to the stereotype of an excellent woman. Among her remarks are the following:

> I rather feel that you're one of those women who shouldn't marry . . . . You seem to me to be somehow *destined* not to marry . . . . I think you'll grow into one of those splendid spinsters—oh, don't think I mean it nastily or cattily—who are pillars of the Church and whom the Church certainly couldn't do without. (194–95)

Sophia's insensitivity is obnoxious and hateful, an index to the tenacity with which people cling to their expectations of others. But it also arises from her conviction that John Challow "isn't the sort of person one would *marry*." Sophia forgets, or does not see as the same sort of thing, that her own marriage to Mark Ainger was considered unsuitable by her mother because he lacked private means. The novel, in fact, is full of unsuitable attachments. Ianthe is quietly scandalized as Sophia chats indulgently about the relationship between her spinster aunt, an elderly, "sinister" figure with dyed hair, and the Italian Dottore of about sixty. Made no more tolerant by her own affection for John, she is shocked again when she makes another charitable call on Miss Grimes and learns she is gone, having married a Polish widower she met in a pub. She and Sophia remind us that our own case or that of someone we love is always different, but perhaps they would be shocked in unison if they knew of the loveless marriage of Ianthe's aunt and uncle, Bertha and Randolph Burdon. Mrs. Burdon almost suggests that if her niece and John "love each other," things might yet be well, but Sophia is not convinced and poses the great conundrum of what they will "talk about in the evenings when the novelty has worn off."

Perhaps they will discuss the kind of thing she chats about with Faustina. By far the most unsuitable attachment ever, from Ianthe's point of view, is Sophia's love for her cat. Senhor MacBride-Pereira observed in *No Fond Return of Love* that "it is only the English who would think of replacing a loved one with an animal." He was wrong, of course, about its being a peculiarly English tendency, but he was right about the importance of the ill-natured Felix, blue-rinsed to match Mrs. Beltane's hair. Sophia's Faustina is entirely spoiled and, though playfully chided from time to time, entirely free to do as she wishes. As far as Sophia is concerned, Faustina is as endlessly fascinating as Christopher Smart's Jeoffry, who "purrs in thankfulness when God tells him he's a good cat." The vicar's household revolves around the pet who is a child substitute and more, "all I've got," according to Sophia:

> I'm the sort of person who wants to do everything for the people I love and [Mark] is the sort of person who's self-sufficient, or seems to be. . . . Then there's Faustina. . . . I feel sometimes that I can't reach Faustina as I've reached other cats. And somehow it's the same with Mark. (99)

The sometimes-disdainful cat is all Sophia has on which she can lavish her love and concern without restraint and without fear of enduring or serious rejection for her excess of emotion. Faustina simply leaps from her arms and no permanent damage is done. Since she gives her "superfluous" love for Mark to Faustina, his quickly suppressed jealousy of the cat when he has Sophia to himself in Rome is understandable. Sophia is unique in the novel only because she focuses on one cat. Edwin Pettigrew, the veterinarian, loves animals and was abandoned by his wife, the marriage "needing more of himself than he could spare from the animals." His sister Daisy, with whom he lives and works, considers it "a real privilege" to feed the animals in their cattery and watches them "with love" while they eat. On the trip to Rome, she carries provisions for the "poor deprived ones," meaning Roman cats. (When some of these disappoint her by being fat and sleek, it is impossible not to remember Ianthe and Miss Grimes.) Nevertheless, Ianthe is offended by Sophia's persistent introduction of Faustina in serious talk, and never more than when the conversation about her possible marriage turns into Sophia's earnest musings that she may have been "wrong to deprive Faustina of the opportunity of motherhood."

We might think it is a pity that this woman cannot channel her extra love into her husband's parish, instead of looking down on the West Indians and "the stupid, ignorant, umbrage-taking members of Mark's congregation." But her love of Faustina, laughable or lamentable though it seems to Ianthe, nevertheless satisfies her will to love. She has made an accommodation to her childlessness and to the personality of the man she loves that gratifies her without harming anyone. As Sophia says, apropos of her marriage to the "other-worldly" vicar, love and its object do not concern anyone but the lover: "*She* is the one who must know in her heart whether he's suitable or not, whatever other people may think." Ianthe can disapprove all she wants of Sophia's love for the independent tortoise-shell cat; it is none of her business and Sophia need not worry about such disapproval—just as Ianthe need not care about her disapproval of John.

In spite of Sophia's fine abstract declaration, when Ianthe's engagement is announced, she still hopes her stereotype will come to life. She and Rupert half-expect, half-hope that John will be discovered to be, as in a Victorian novel, an "impostor." Never mind that Ianthe would suffer as the deceived woman; only by being alone can she still conform to the pattern of the excellent woman, "destined" to spinsterhood. But when Sophia meets John, he is all devotion and tells her he hopes to "fit into the parish as Ianthe's husband."

Rupert is more fortunate. A rare flash of insight into his own feelings descends upon him as he speaks to the bride and groom:

> A formal and meaningless speech, he reflected, but had his relationship with Ianthe ever been more than that? He had been slow to seize his opportunities, but had he ever really wanted to get anywhere with her? A line of poetry came into his mind, something about a garland of red roses on the habit of a nun—loving her might have been like that. (253–54)

"It would have seemed like living his life backwards," as he thinks in another context, if he had chosen an image of his mother to love. Fortunately, one man's mother superior is another man's passionate ideal, and there is no indication that Ianthe reminds John of those stern, forbiddingly chaste figures. To Rupert, Penelope seems neither sisterly nor motherly. He has another impression of the vulnerability so appealing to him when he notices that she marks the gala of Ianthe's wedding with false eyelashes too thick for clear vision. As usual when faced with the pathos he alone sees, he decides to make a romantic move, the conventional one of taking a girl out after a wedding. But, as usual, by the time he gets around to it, it is too late. Penny has left, which so upsets him that he suspects a plot framed by the sisters "on purpose to spite him." Determined as he is, finally, to pursue Penny, he cannot afford to overindulge in umbrage, and he does not wait too long to surprise her at her office. He arrives after she has already gone out to lunch. We begin to wonder, like Jane Cleveland and Andrew Marvell, "What object could Fate possibly have in enviously debarring love" between Penelope and this excellent (though maladroit) man? But at last he catches sight of her and decides to approach her "carefully and not say anything to annoy or upset her." Tears, he feels, would be unsuitable to early afternoon in St. Paul's churchyard.

*   *   *

Rupert's cautious but determined approach toward Penelope, a man in deliberate but slightly apprehensive pursuit of a woman, is a good image to keep in mind as we consider some of the emotional and behavioral similarities that link Pym's men and women in the four novels we have discussed. The need to love unites characters as different as Rupert Stonebird and Catherine Oliphant, John Challow and Wilmet Forsyth, Sophia Ainger and Keith, Daisy Pettigrew and Harry Talbot; shaping their thoughts and underlying their actions, love matters to all of them whether or not they deliberate about it as such. Men and women of all ages concede, at least implicitly, the necessity of love; it does not occur to people like Sybil Forsyth and Arnold Root and Aunt Hermione and her vicar that the younger people around them will think their marriages slightly ridiculous. For some, like Aylwin Forbes and Wilmet Forsyth, the need to be admired or loved outweighs or equals the need to love, but insofar as this desire is a factor in their attitudes and behavior, it too declares the importance of love.

Many of Pym's characters enjoy observing others, and

some even do it as part of their work. It is an ordinary activity when it indicates a human interest or attachment on the part of the observer. Senhor MacBride-Pereira and Rhoda Wellcome, living quiet lives as members of their communities, are happy with this supplement to their personal involvement. Their desire to know about the lives of others is a form of involvement with their community. Rupert Stonebird and Catherine Oliphant cultivate detachment as a defensive attitude, the former to cover his shyness and the latter to deal with pain. But observation can also signal detachment, the separation of the observer from his subjects, and Pym emphasizes the threat of such alienation. Dulcie Mainwaring admits that her "researches" add zest to her relatively dull life but is not sure she is ready to settle for living alone on the sidelines. Alaric Lydgate is an unwilling observer, lonely because his shyness and fearfulness separate him from others. Most miserable is Tom Mallow. When detached observation becomes his habitual stance at home as in the field, he is alienated from all the ties that made him a whole person. Tom makes the cowardly choice when he fails to heed the message of his various dissatisfactions and confusions. His fate suggests the meaning of such detachment in Pym's novels.

Lacking conventional objects for emotional fulfillment, those of Pym's people who are more fortunate than Tom turn to various options. The pet is the substitute love-object discussed as such by the characters most often, probably because such affection is manifested more readily and more openly than others. (There are no babies in Pym's world, except offstage.) Mrs. Beltane, Sophia, and the Pettigrews seem ridiculous to some of their friends, but it does not lessen their attachment to their animals or diminish the gratification they derive from having something to love. Familial ties are fundamental to the lives of Rhoda Wellcome and Mabel Swan. Like these sisters but to a greater degree, Dulcie's Aunt Hermione and Uncle Bertram needle and annoy each other, rubbing along together in intimate disharmony until their hearts' desires, the vicarage and the monastery, beckon at last. Mervyn Cantrell is all for his mother, and Daisy and Edwin Pettigrew manage together at home and in the veterinary office. In the absence of family, sympathetic friends pair off, people like Esther Clovis and Gertrude Lydgate, and Augusta Prideaux and Sir Denbigh Grote. The last pair interests Wilmet as being socially mismatched: a former governess and a retired diplomat who enjoy each other's companionship because they share memories of the same events, places, and people, though from different perspectives. It does not matter. As the basis for relationship, a shared past, a similar background, a mutual love of animals, an academic discipline, a common faith, an occupation or interest—any one will do; the bases for connection between Pym's characters are as varied as the people who have or make them and, as even Wilmet understands, the important thing is to make them.

A more frequent alternative to emotional isolation is the unsuitable attachment, and here we see very clearly the development from the earlier novels. Men as often as women seek out or succumb to objects unsuitable on various grounds, and the extramarital interests of Harry Talbot and Wilmet and Rodney Forsyth are only the most obvious. We mentioned the various examples in *No Fond Return of Love* and *An Unsuitable Attachment*. In these two novels, the reader realizes more readily than the characters the irrelevance to love of the standard criteria of suitability or unsuitability, questions of class, background, economic status, and age. The matter is discussed by Sophia Ainger and Ianthe Broome after they witness Harriet Bede's obvious affection for Basil Branche, and their conversation leads to an interesting distinction. Sophia speaks for the author in the declaration that the person who loves must be the one to decide questions of suitability, "whatever other people may think." But when it comes to the point with Ianthe about John Challow, the distinction Sophia makes between "just" loving someone unsuitable (which cannot be wrong) and doing something tangible about it (which cannot be right) strikes us as muddled because her judgmental distinction is inappropriate in the context of Ianthe and John. It is not the case, as we see in these novels, that people can monitor and control their feelings for each other according to suitability. What they can and should control, according to Sophia (and to Dulcie Mainwaring when she scolds Aylwin), is their behavior. But the suitability of particular expressions of love can also be determined only by those involved and, in Pym's world, one can depend on their essential decency and sense of propriety to guide them: Harriet coddles Basil, Wilmet flirts with Piers, Harry flirts with Wilmet, and Rodney flirts with Prudence Bates. These people are irreproachable on account of their "unsuitable" feelings—everyone needs "little bits of romance"—and draw back in guilt, if it ever gets to that point, from what they consider unsuitable behavior. Within these self-imposed restraints, Pym's people find gratification in forms and degrees satisfactory to themselves. In Pym's novels there is no attachment that is "unsuitable" in the sense in which her characters use the word. What is unsuitable between men and women is a relationship not based on love (like the marriage of Bertha and Randolph Burdon or the marriage Mervyn Cantrell proposes for himself and Ianthe's furniture) or a relationship based on a craven desire for superiority (like Tom's attraction to Deirdre or Aylwin's taste for "girl-wives").

The imaginative transformation by people of those they love or want to love is evident in Aylwin's "Fanny Price" and Rupert's "Pre-Raphaelite beatnik." Of more interest is the male imagination at work in the creation of women as a class different from themselves. The men in Pym's earlier novels were not much interested in the sex as a whole, simply assuming the existence of a secondary and serviceable group. In these books, as women achieve prominence in the world outside the home, the masculine absent-minded and patronizing indulgence gives way to more competitive attitudes. Some men like Tom Mallow, Aylwin Forbes, and Rodney Forsyth feel threatened by women whose accomplishments or attitudes parallel their own: Tom resents Catherine's interest in her own work and denies its importance or significance; Aylwin scorns women whose intelligence might outstrip and supplant his in common work; and Rodney denies femininity to women who find fulfillment in careers. Confronted by attitudes and activities reflecting their own, they fail to perceive them as similarities or to value them as they do in themselves; instead, they imagine Woman as a creature different from themselves, unattractive in her priorities, foolish in her aspirations, and threatening in her abilities.

116

Women continue, as in the earlier novels, to respond to the needs and vulnerabilities they perceive in others, and some of the men in these middle novels have acquired similar sensitivities. They too base their emotional lives on the needs or vulnerabilities they perceive in people who interest them. Catherine wants to help Alaric Lydgate, and Digby Fox is ready to console Deirdre. Wilmet's desire to help Piers straighten out what seems to be an unhappy life is shared by Keith, and her idea that there is something sad about Piers is echoed in his idea about Keith: "Yes—imagine it, Wilmet. The pathos of anyone not knowing French—I mean, not at all!" Ianthe's interest in John grows from her awareness of his poverty, and Rupert Stonebird's in Penelope from his notion of her little errors in appearance or comportment. They both make a deliberate unconventional choice based on their parallel sympathies. On a larger scale, the feelings of sympathy and compassion for others that inspire Pym's feminine do-gooders now move men as well: Bill Coleman, a dedicated churchworker, dislikes Wilf Bason but helps to rectify the situation about the Faberge egg; Mark Ainger feels called to work in what Sophia considers a low-class area with low-class people. As Wilmet sees for her fastidious self, the "burden-bearing type" includes men and women "of all types and ages."

As men pursue love, they sometimes feel subjected by their needs to little assaults on their dignity:

> The things women did to men! Had anyone ever really made a serious study of the subject, of the innumerable pinpricks and humiliations endured by men at the hands of women? (*NFR*, 83)

Aylwin's sentiments echo Mildred Lathbury's as she strolls past the Learned Society and Rupert Stonebird's as he fumes about "The Wiles of Nice Women in a Civilised Society." Yet in acting to fulfill their needs to love and be loved, all of Pym's major characters in these novels affirm their individual worth and dignity. With the exception of Tom Mallow, who chooses academic curiosity over personal development and scholarly detachment over human involvement, Pym's men and women anticipate or find fulfillment of a kind that satisfies and nourishes their emotional lives.

IV. Failure and Reprise

Anyone who turns to *The Sweet Dove Died* or to *Quartet in Autumn* expecting one of Pym's sharp but essentially positive comedies is in for a shock. In these novels, Pym brings an extraordinary power to her depiction of the solitary existence, whether emotional isolation is the result of an egotistical choice (as it is in the first novel) or the consequence of a real inability to reach out to others (as it is in the second).

Most of the previous novels are affirmations: focusing on the desire or ability of diverse people to find emotional sustenance in different situations, they celebrate the various kinds of love and affection and, most of all, the triumph of the spirit in choosing connection. From the beginning, however, Pym realized the potential for tragedy in many of her characters' lives: imagine Belinda Bede (as she imagines herself at one point) without her sister, or Harriet alone and falling in love seriously and for the first time with a youthful curate. Mrs. Bone, Everard's mother, with her insane notion that the birds are out to get her, is funny because her friend Miss Jessop, her son, and her economic situation protect her from total isolation despite her eccentricities. Senhor MacBride-Pereira, without Mrs. Beltane's friendship or house as his base for observation, and she without Felix, would not amuse Dulcie or the reader. Miss Grimes, in whom Ianthe expects to find misery, might have been a sad case: happiness seems unlikely for a retired woman completely alone and living in a boarding house. Instead, she is a source of humor because she obviously is not miserable or alone, especially when it turns out that she has found a husband in the Four Feathers, the pub she frequents. Augusta Prideaux without the special friendship of Sir Denbigh Grote (or vice versa) and without the help of friends like Sybil Forsyth would be a pathetic figure—but these emotional props gain her admission into the comic world, a community where no serious harm can befall her.

Crampton Hodnet, *Jane and Prudence*, and especially *Less Than Angels* indicate a different perspective. Francis Cleveland's desire for feeling and for confirmation of his existence as a significant person, though finally undermined by Pym's uncertainties, are pitiable; they suggest, though imperfectly, the effects of lovelessness and the lengths to which people will go to satisfy their need to matter emotionally to someone. More clearly than this, Prudence Bates's self-centered inability to commit herself in love to anyone and Tom Mallow's choice of detachment are the materials of the tragic novelist. None of these three figures, however, define the novels they appear in as tragic or even as very somber. Francis loses the dream of romantic love with Barbara Bird but falls back into the bosom of Margaret and his community, which is less than ideal but very much better than nothing. Prudence, at twenty-nine, is still too young for her failures to seem desperate or incapable of some kind of improvement; therefore, it is unpleasant to learn, in *A Glass of Blessings*, that she broke an engagement to Edward Lyall and sees men like the married Rodney Forsyth. Tom Mallow's death is vaguely sad but it averts real tragedy, which would be the necessity of living with his self-chosen isolation.

An older version of Prudence stands before us in Leonora Eyre, and characters like Mrs. Bone, Miss Grimes, Senhor MacBride-Pereira, Tom Mallow, and the others contribute to the identities of Marcia, Letty, Edwin, and Norman. Before turning to Pym's last novel and the comic reprise of her thematic concerns, we will consider the fates of people no longer young who belong to no supportive community and who do not or cannot make the emotional connections vital to life. Though *The Sweet Dove Died* and *Quartet in Autumn* are tragic and *A Few Green Leaves* is not, Pym's last three novels are about the failure to recognize the need for love.

The Sweet Dove Died

Pym's comic novels remind us persistently of imperfection, the little and larger blotches in the world, in relationships, in others, and in ourselves. Most of us, like Pym's characters, accommodate ourselves to this state of affairs in order to live comfortably, peaceably, and sociably with others and with ourselves, and in order to love and be loved.

But heroes, saints, reformers, misfits, unbalanced individuals, and other such solitary figures remind us that there are those who will not or can not accommodate themselves to the conditions most of us take for granted. In *The Sweet Dove Died*, Pym explores the character and fate of Leonora Eyre, a woman obsessed with perfection in objects, in herself, and in relationships. The novel centers on her relationship with James Boyce; it is about the testing of Leonora, as first love and then misery present her with the choice of joining or rejecting the imperfect world and human race. In addition to issues of perfection and accommodation, the novel particularly focuses on possessive romantic love, on asexual forms of love, and on the emotional options available to fulfill the need for love; finally, it raises the question of which is greater, the need to love or the need to be loved.

Leonora seems inhumanly cold, proud, elegant, and controlled to most of the people who know her. Dickie Murray starts his wife giggling by suggesting that he continually feels he would like to attack their friend sexually. So impossible is it for them to see Leonora as a sexual creature that merely mentioning the possibility of her sleeping with Humphrey Boyce sends them off into more laughter. A neighbor knows Leonora better from spending occasional evenings with her. Typically, Liz begins their get-togethers with the story of unhappiness, divorce, and anger that explains her embittered alienation from men. Leonora responds with her tale of happiness in childhood and in many subsequent romantic attachments that seem pointless to her friend. Liz is just as bored by this recitation as Leonora is by hers, but finally "each woman would feel a kind of satisfaction, as if more than just drink and food had been offered and accepted." Satisfaction derives from a similarity apparent to neither woman. The details of their plots differ, but they exchange the same information: each tells what led her, at this point of her life, to be alone, without the conventional kinds of love that bind most people to others. Liz does not understand the meaning of Leonora's seemingly self-enhancing tale of serial, inconclusive romances, but she understands the lovelessness that determined it better than the Murrays. Eventually, she almost wants her elegant friend to get hurt so that she can "find out whether it was possible for the cold, proud, and well-organized Leonora to suffer."

Near fifty as the novel opens, Leonora is good-looking enough to attract Humphrey and James Boyce and to strike an observant stranger like Senhor MacBride-Pereira (*NFR*) as beautiful. Still, she is best seen in her own setting with its subdued lighting. Well-preserved though she is, fifty is fifty, and strain, weariness, and strong sunlight occasionally reveal the tiny lines and wrinkles that must mar, as far as she is concerned, the perfection of her appearance. Rare tears come to her eyes at the sight of age spots on her hands. Leonora looks back on younger days remarkable for that steady succession of flirtations. She cannot sympathize with Liz's complaints because "she had never been badly treated or rejected by a man—perhaps she had never loved another person with enough intensity for such a thing to be possible." She has not even experienced romantic love because "something had invariably been not quite right." The Murrays' idea that sex is unthinkable for her is almost accurate: she tried it a few times, disliked it, and is hugely relieved to assume that, at her age, she need never do it again. Though she realizes (quite contentedly) that she has known little emotion and no passion in her life, she likes to think of it as "calm of mind, all passion spent, or, more rarely, as emotion recollected in tranquility."

Leonora can quote Milton or Wordsworth but the fact remains: she is a cold woman, and her attitude toward sex is the least of her problems. She cannot bear to be touched by men or women, sees Liz and Meg as "foils" for herself, scoffs at their emotional problems, pities them for the accommodations they have made in their lives, and scorns the inoffensive Miss Foxe, remarking that old people, if encouraged by friendliness, "encroach." "What do you *do*?" a stranger challenges her at a cocktail party: Leonora does not work, volunteer, go to church, garden, play bridge—she does not do much of anything because she has no interests beyond maintaining the elegance of her person and her house. She disdains to tell the stranger her favorite pastimes: examining for imperfections, washing, and polishing her tasteful bric-a-brac. This, shopping, and maintaining her own appearance seem to be the chief occupations of a woman who exists for two reasons: to excite the admiration of her acquaintances and of a little troop of "elderly admirers," and to admire herself for meeting her own high standards for her personal and emotional styles. The emptiness of her life is as remarkable as her seeming contentment with it. We are not surprised to learn that she has pills for stress on her night table and suffers from migraines.

It is ironic and pathetic that the one love this proud woman experiences should be for a bisexual man, her junior by twenty-five years. Of all people, and with the perfectly suitable Humphrey in attendance, Leonora's heart chooses James. At first, his flattering admiration, like his antique mirror, shows her the reflection of a "fascinating and ageless" woman. Pym gives us, in the fruitwood mirror decorated with Cupids, the perfect image elucidating Leonora's love of James. As it recurs, it reminds us of Donne's image of the beloved's eyes as "glasses," and the reminder suggests the psychological accuracy of Pym's observation about love. What Leonora experiences with James, and for the first time, is an objective, external view of herself in a guise that charms her and coincides with how she wishes to be seen— the mirror shows her the "ageless" woman that James actually sees in the first flush of affection. James *sees* Leonora and she sees that he does. She loves him for the impression she senses she has made on him, for the reflection she sees in his eyes and his mirror—though she knows the glass has "some slight flaw in it," and that it shows the ageless woman if she places it "in a certain light."

For James, the basis of the attraction is more simple: he has recently lost his mother, to whom he was very close, and feels more comfortable as a rule with older women. Moreover, he is relatively inexperienced sexually and not sure how he feels about the signals other men flash his way; obviously, Leonora poses no threat to his sexual uncertainty. She is vaguely cognizant that "if his mother *hadn't* died . . .," he might not pursue the relationship with her, but beyond thinking that a young man's interest is an appropriate tribute to herself, she does not analyze her own interest and growing attachment. A handsome young man might appeal to anyone, but he is precisely what Leonora, with her frigid standoffishness, wants. James is attentive and affectionate without giving or expecting physical caresses beyond the social, occasional kiss on the cheek. Leonora never admits it, but her frequent remarks to James that she does not think of him as a "man," and eventually her unsurprised reaction to Ned, suggest that she thinks he is homosexual. Given her distaste for physical affection, his possible homosexuality is a positive attraction. At first, the relationship beckons her as an unexpected repetition of the inconclusive but delightful flirtations of her past. After all, James is not someone for whom love could become real, in the sense of entailing passion or of leading to anything permanent. It is an unstable situation from the start, as Leonora says she knows, because it is to be expected that a young man of twenty-four will find other attachments.

Leonora, who so craves admiration, comes to need James's in particular. More importantly, his unthreatening and undemanding affection sparks a response in her the more ferocious for lying dormant for so long. The entirety of her capacity to love, focused exclusively on him, grows riotously, and as James discovers other interests, she imperceptibly becomes the lover and he the beloved. Though James regards and treats her with such gallantry as might be accorded a doting mother by an extremely devoted son, there is nothing particularly "maternal" about her emotions: this physically and emotionally frigid person especially (and irrationally) cherishes James as proof of her womanly attractiveness and desirability. She considers theirs the "perfect" relationship and eventually fantasizes that they might marry, "very quietly," of course. As unsuitable, unreal, unnatural, and perverse as it seems to Humphrey (or to anyone else), Leonora loves James. The experience of loving and then losing him alters her a bit and gives her, ultimately, the opportunity to change herself and her life radically. Pym emphasizes Leonora's emotional options, represented in her friends' lives; any one of them might redeem her.

Leonora's friendship with James grows so precipitously because she literally has had nothing else but herself and her objects. As it develops and she looks outward, toward him, she forgets herself from time to time, such small moments being the more important for being so unusual. The knowledge that she is admired by an attractive and desirable young man gives her a wonderful bonus. The narcissistic woman feels secure enough to make a running joke with him of the spectacles she hid in the past ("one's failing sight, so middle-aged"), and to challenge him flirtatiously when he refers to a dress she wears as "autumnall": "You mean that I look old? That I'm in the autumn of life?" Made "ageless," in her own eyes, by his interest, Leonora enjoys a measure of security in James's acceptance of her "imperfections." She also feels "increasingly curious" about Meg's relationship with Colin, an alliance she previously regarded as pitiable and almost contemptible, and accepts an invitation she was inclined to reject in order to learn what she can. One evening when she is suffering from one of her headaches and disappointed because she cannot reach James, Meg calls and Leonora surmises that she must also be alone. The curiosity about her friend's relationship and the comparison Leonora makes between Meg and herself first suggest her underlying assumption about James's sexuality; but they also imply her unconscious awareness that her situation is not unique, an insight whose realization could be of great value to her.

All is well until Leonora learns of James's relationship with Phoebe Sharpe. From his point of view, Phoebe throws herself at him, so that he hardly knows how they end up in bed together, but he pursues the acquaintance, enjoying it especially as his "secret" from Leonora and Humphrey, the two adults who seem to control his life. It seems a mild enough rebellion, but it reveals the nature of Leonora's love. Until she hears of Phoebe's existence, she is entirely content with James. Obviously, she has been getting what she wants from him and has noticed nothing amiss in their friendship. Moreover, since James is out of the country, she is free to characterize his affair to herself as she wishes, and concludes immediately that it is "sordid and unworthy, the kind of liaison James would be ashamed of and that meant very little to him." Her first reaction after the initial shock is to minimize his sexual involvement with a young woman as something that cannot touch his relationship with her. If she could have rested in this confident perspective or considered her options, she might have survived her first test with some grace.

But Leonora cannot be like James's uncle. Humphrey admires and courts Leonora from the first, but as he gets to know her, he has no illusions about her "perfection." Little things like her choice of an unflattering color, her invention of "favourite sights" on the spot, and her fondness for *Tosca* are noted by Humphrey, but tolerantly and affectionately, each the "tiny flaw in her perfection that made her human." Even if Humphrey did not see these small things as imperfections in the woman he wants, he could not miss her most glaring "flaw," her odd preference for his twenty-four-year-old nephew. He is at first willing to see it as a maternal affection, but over time he comes to see it more truly as a romantic attachment, characterizing it to her as "unnatural" and to himself as "perverse." If Humphrey and Leonora are the parent substitutes against whom James feels the urge to rebel, Humphrey is involved in a submerged but bizarre Oedipal situation, competing against and resenting the "son" who has taken his rightful place with the mother-figure in the psychic skit. Yet, beyond informing on his nephew and Phoebe, telling Leonora how unsuitable her preference is, and making an unwelcome lunge at her, Humphrey does nothing drastic. He is content to wait, to take what Leonora gives him, living in the hope that his imperfect lady will turn to him when she comes to her senses and sees him as her appropriate swain. He really is, with his patience, understanding, and solicitude, more than appropriate, and his behavior represents one of Leonora's options.

For Leonora, James's imperfection is his ability to roam, his openness to other, "unworthy" attachments. Miss Culver's remark about how just when you think men are "close they suddenly go off" brings her possessiveness to the surface:

> She hardly liked to admit it, but she did sometimes feel slightly uneasy when James was out of her sight and this business with Phoebe Sharpe—whether there had been much or little in it— showed that her anxiety was justified. (119)

That anxiety inspires her, immediately after learning about Phoebe from Humphrey, to take the first step in moving

Miss Foxe out so she can move James in. (Fortunately, the unwanted tenant is eager to vacate, having heard of a church-operated house for the elderly from Sophia Ainger.) The lengths to which Leonora goes to get his furniture from Phoebe are ludicrous, but she is intent on demonstrating that nothing of James belongs to the young woman. Wresting a few inconsequential oddments from her is merely a convenient way to make the point. She cannot emulate Humphrey.

The ease with which Leonora vanquishes Phoebe and moves the absent James into the flat in her own house reassures her, and her security in love again finds outward expression. When she buys the expensive pair of porcelain vases for James's birthday surprise (after doublechecking that they are quite flawless), a little thought inspires her to speak kindly to the clerk she has been treating icily: "a ridiculous tag or motto . . . something about passing through this world but once and therefore taking care to be kind to a fellow creature." Dismissing the idea as "absurd," she still makes her tiny effort and, as a consequence of her thought for another, is led to a bit of self-awareness, a glimpse of the disparity between what others see and what she believes she is. She wonders whether she seems "so cold, proud and formidable" to others when she is "none of these things." Certainly, the whole tussle with Phoebe demonstrated her vulnerability and a lapse of pride, and other uncharacteristic feelings and actions indicate her potential for change. The woman who hates physical contact throws herself into James's arms when he comes home, and she even begins to think she might enjoy caresses—his, at least.

It might seem that "Love calls" Leonora, at last, "to the things of this world," and to an extent it does. But we cannot ignore the context of possessiveness in which her potential for change unfolds. In pre-Phoebe days, she was more than pleased that James gave no unpleasant sign of bodily affection, and her fantasy of marriage, originating after her reflection on Miss Culver's disquieting statement, assumed that "of course dear James wouldn't expect anything like that" distasteful physicality. Her new receptiveness toward sex may be a part of her effort to bind him to herself more securely—if what he wants is what Phoebe gave him, then Leonora, in her desire to hold him by being everything to him, is willing to give him that. On the other hand, it might be an aspect of the slow but general unthawing James has instigated. In either case, her changed attitude indicates the strength of her love for James and the extent to which she prizes his affection.

The bars on the windows that discomfit James are only the first sign of his uneasiness about their situation. He begins to feel mastered by her, defeated by everything from her retrieval of his furniture to her tactful understanding. Inhibited even in his cooking by her presence downstairs, he resents her spending time with Liz one evening when he would like a late cup of tea with her. It is not just the remark he overhears ("But, darling, one would hardly wish to be a mother to somebody like *that*!") that upsets him; it is his unarticulated awareness that Leonora has taken so much—his freedom and his independence—from him that he feels she owes him at least her company when and if he happens to want it. The porcelain vases he had so much wanted no longer appeal very much as a birthday present from Leonora. The amount of money he knows they cost seems as excessive as her emotions, and James feels like a child with a sick stomach from the surfeit of her overindulgent love. Nothing is more embarrassing and uncomfortable than great displays of unwanted love.

It would be easy to see the malicious Ned purely as a troublemaker, especially since he comes to confront Leonora in her own house. But she made the first move when she chose to imprison James in the lovely flat above her; before they ever met, her ill-considered action made her Ned's antagonist. As the brash American, he is the irrepressible spirit of independence that will not permit James to be taken without a good fight. Leonora thinks, after she has her young man where she wants him, that she is being "good" by not prying or taking too much of his time. But it is like giving her inmate yard privileges, or to use Keats's metaphor, like weaving a string long enough to permit the dove's flight around an entire room. In his captivity, James had begun to think

Leonora was all-powerful, but he took comfort in the thought that she would not find Ned as easy to subdue. When his friend comes charging into the luncheon with which Leonora planned to incorporate Ned into her design, it becomes evident even to her that she is being incorporated into his. Looking in Ned's eyes, Leonora sees a new, unattractive reflection of herself and everyone else: "the glitter of his personality [made] Leonora seem no more than an ageing overdressed woman, Liz a shrewish nonentity, and James and Humphrey a callow young man with his pompous uncle." Obviously, James sees something different, which inspires him to root for the lover "who claimed all his attention in a way that the women never had."

Leonora's first experience of suffering for someone she loves, of being "badly treated or rejected by a man," begins the moment she meets and recognizes Ned as the "something she had always been afraid of in her relationship with James." Her anguish as she tries and fails to outmaneuver her antagonist is palpable, and her reaction is an imperfect attempt to retreat into her former self. As she begins to control herself into appearing coolly unaffected, the novel takes on a breathless, claustrophobic quality. Even James, faced with her show of equanimity and unconcern, wishes several times she would make a scene, some tangible human sign of her unhappiness. She does not. The contempt she feels for the unaccompanied woman she sees at Keats's house turns very quickly into envy of someone who seems content and unburdened in her solitude. She is upset that Meg might realize she has been neglected and made miserable by James, and keeps up the proud pretense that everything is well. But she decides she might bestow a kiss on Humphrey when he comes to dinner. However, he leaves early, and without even trying for that rare kiss, after announcing James's intention to move into another flat. Beneath Leonora's rigid control, the pain implodes with such force that she is disappointed by Humphrey's departure:

> She felt now as if she had been cheated of something, a warmer show of affection, the kiss she had expected and had decided to allow him. They might even have ended up in bed and it could have been cosy and comforting for her. (167–68)

Nothing could more clearly indicate her desperate need for comfort.

James takes his fruitwood mirror, naturally, when he goes, and the discovery is awful to Leonora, but worse follows from the realization that he has dropped her. His abandonment plunges her to the nadir of her misery. As love did, suffering brings her little glimpses of a world beyond herself, and her experience enables her to empathize with the vulnerability of others, albeit in a comparatively superficial sense. Alone, looking at antique jewelry at Christie's, she realizes the extent of her unhappiness and is moved to tears "not only for herself but also for the owners of the jewellery, ageing now or old, some probably dead." When she takes refuge in a coffee shop she had visited with James, the elderly waitress whom he had called "the Polish countess" looks older and more fragile now than she had remembered. The authenticity of her sympathy is not compromised by the superficial values informing it: Leonora assumes that age, no less than death, strips the individual of beauty and romance, and it is this loss whose sorrow overwhelms her. From identifying with nameless, old strangers who have shed their embellishments with their youth, and with a woman older than herself whose features suggest a former grandeur, she descends to the tray of trash the waitress rests on her table:

> Leonora was conscious that she herself belonged here too, with the sad jewellery and the old woman and the air of things that had seen better days. Even the cast-off crusts, the ruined cream cakes and the cigarette ends had their significance. (184)

James's abandonment has revealed her spiritual emptiness. Before Leonora loved James and felt loved, the image she saw in mirrors, though the construct of pride and self-centeredness, was a facade she could approve and admire. Loved by James, she saw the fantasy-come-true of ageless fascination. But the razing of that wondrous image destroys the facade too, and she now sees something used, ruined, and superfluous. Leonora is a foolish and pathetic woman not because she loved unwisely or because, predictably, she has been abandoned, but because she has no conception of her own dignity and especially of her dignity as a loving woman: her love has not died, after all. But she believes James's has—and being unloved makes Leonora trash in her own eyes.

She feels "debased, diminished" and "utterly alone," but pride stifles the urge to confide in her cousin Daphne. Self-defeating pride also rules out the acceptability of taking Liz's option. Embittered against all men because of her bad marriage, Liz breeds and shows Siamese cats and, as Leonora says, loves "cats more than people." Sophia Ainger, Daisy, Edwin Pettigrew (*UA*), and Mrs. Beltane (*NFR*) could understand this. Edwin's failure to hold his wife and his great success with animals reminded us of one of the virtues of the latter: relationships with them are not nearly as demanding, complicated, or emotionally risky as human affairs. Yet, since they involve communication and interaction, they are relationships: like their human counterparts, animals enable a person to express the self and to see its external reflection. Mrs. Beltane, looking in Felix's beady eyes, sees a loving woman still needed despite the death of her husband and the independence of her children. Faustina shows Sophia a woman with too much love, not an unflattering image by any means, and Liz's cats enable her to see herself as a nurturing and loving woman. Directly after Leonora leaves Daphne, one of her friend's cats confronts her:

> She tried to send it back over the wall but the animal would not go and continued to weave around her uttering its mournful cries. What did it want? She felt she ought to say something to it, but she could never distinguish Liz's cats by name, and "Pussy" seemed altogether too feeble and inadequate a form of address. As she puzzled, Liz came to the wall. . . . One would hardly want to be like the people who fill the emptiness of their lives with an animal, Leonora thought, going back into the house. (188)

For just a moment a small impulse almost moves her to respond, but Leonora cannot take Liz's imperfect option.

Spring finds Leonora feeling somehow revitalized though "it seemed as if a part of her had died" during the winter of James's absence. She is not quite the same. Being alone no longer gives her pleasure, and she almost enjoys spending time with Liz or Meg. She feels no pleasure, either, in the "kind of victory" she wins by staying in control during Ned's visit to return James to her officially. However, when the long-suppressed breakdown occurs as a great but brief burst of sobs, embarrassment and shame are simultaneous with her sobs, and she finds "the contact" of Meg's hug "distasteful." All she can think of while her friend comforts and advises her is how "ridiculous Meg looked, kneeling there on the floor." James's anticipated return is no less awkward. Hoping to resume their relationship after the hiatus, he believes she will always be there for him, "like one's mother." Asking Leonora's forgiveness, he offers Ned's rejection of himself to her simply, as his defenselessness and openness and as a pain akin to her own. She knows "that with this confidence she was receiving more from him than she ever had before," but she can make no answering gesture of reconciliation.

At the critical moment when James asks, "Where do we go from here?," Leonora thinks of Meg and Colin. Meg has never been a woman Leonora admires. From her casual approach to her appearance to her love for a young homosexual man, Meg seems thoroughly unappealing and pitiable to her. The relationship of the older woman with the younger man follows a cyclical course. Meg and Colin are close, enjoying their mutual devotion, until he falls in love with another man. At some point during this relationship, he disappears and she suffers and waits for his return. Eventually he comes back, and reconciliation is celebrated over a bottle of his favorite wine from Meg's refrigerator, at which point the cycle starts again. This relationship might seem pitiable or crazy to Leonora, but Meg learns love from it. A woman doctor explains to her eventually about the need to love and the usefulness of "a sort of child substitute," but Meg does not need validation or instruction in what she feels and knows. She loves Colin, values his companionship above anyone else's, and enjoys pleasing him. Because she loves him, she accepts his friends, accepts her role in his life as the stable, unchanging friend, and accepts the imperfection in the relationship—his habit of disappearing periodically. The relationship with Colin demands a vocabulary new to her, and she uses it, though she finds it hard to refer to Colin's "lover," and though she can say "you have to let people be free" only in a "brave manner."

Though she could not admit it until she cried before her friend, Leonora has lived part of Meg's experience, losing James to Ned and dealing with an immense hurt while she waited for him to come back. Meg spoke to her then of "the need to accept people as they are and to love them whatever they did." In a perfect world of perfect people, Meg would not need a "child substitute" in the first place, and it would not be necessary to make allowances for people or their behavior. Things being as they are, Meg wisely advises her friend, "You mustn't expect things to be perfect, Leonora, they never are."

As James stands uncertainly before Leonora, Meg and Colin reenact their reconciliation in her mind. Of all things, an imaginary bottle of wine, the bottle she imagines Meg keeps handy for reconciliations, paralyzes her: "there was something humiliating about the idea of wooing James in this way, like an animal being enticed back into its cage." Her simile sketches a complete scene: the hunter, the prey, the bait, and the cage. Leonora's implied image simultaneously defines Meg's role and suggests her own distaste for being the pursuer: James may approach her, but he is the one with the urge to fly. Her image diminishes Meg, Colin, James, and the basic human needs that move them and bring them together, however imperfectly; but what repels her is what she sees as the diminishment of self. She is moved not by self-respect but by the shabby notion that it is shameful and degrading to show emotional need and to accept what is less than perfect. Dismissing James, Leonora chooses not to be like Meg.

Ironically, the image with which she unconsciously debases the others reveals her as the pitiable one. A conciliatory gesture from her *would* be bait because she still thinks in terms of possessing James, of snaring him in a cage. He would have to want to escape not because he is "an animal" of a different nature but because of the possessive nature of her love. Leonora's sole experience of love, with its potential to work radical changes, is a dead end because of her ineradicable self-centeredness and passion for perfection. Unlike Humphrey, she cannot accept imperfection in another; unlike Liz, she cannot accept an imperfect substitute as the object of her affection; and unlike Meg, she cannot accept an imperfect relationship. Having rejected the options available to her, she retreats to perfect objects, some of which the faithful Humphrey (who deserves better) gives her.

> The sight of such large and faultless blooms, so exquisite in colour, so absolutely correct in all their finer points, was a comfort and satisfaction to one who loved perfection as she did. Yet, when one came to think of it, the only flowers that were really perfect were those, like the peonies that went so well with one's charming room, that possessed the added grace of having been presented to oneself. (208)

For Meg and Liz, the need to love is primary, but not for Leonora. The dove, the "something" that died during her painful winter, was her desire and willingness to love. She prefers to be the object of her own admiration.

Quartet in Autumn

In *Quartet in Autumn*, Pym continues her exploration of lovelessness, but from a different, bleaker angle than the one she chose for *The Sweet Dove Died*. Leonora chooses not to love, but at fifty and with people like Humphrey, Liz, and Meg around, she has no frightening sense of futility, of total isolation. For Letty, Edwin, Norman, and especially for Marcia, the central character of this novel, the situation is considerably grimmer: each is really alone, and not necessarily by choice. In their sixties, at or close to retirement age, they are threatened by total isolation in London, the big impersonal city that could be any other in its anonymity and coldness. It is a world made filthy with the scrawls of large, anonymous hatreds ("Kill Asian Shit"), of underground trains in which wisdom is to ignore the occasional figure collapsed in some stage of illness or need. There is no small community within the larger city to claim the individual members of the quartet, and they have no circle of friends. At their age, they seem to have very few options or none at all.

The novel deals especially with the gradual deterioration of Marcia Ivory, as she moves further into mental imbalance and starves herself to death in spite of the many eyes being kept on her. Its central purpose is to show how desperate is the need for the connection of individuals by responsibility, the responsibility the Bible calls love. The central conflict, carefully ignored by all, is whether to do something about Marcia or to keep clear of the situation. It is not a simple conflict. Marcia resists most efforts made to help her, and the people around her are average, decent types, governed by reservations and ideas most readers will recognize: it is better not to get involved; there is no need to worry about people in these days of the welfare state; some people do not want help and certainly cannot be forced to accept it—the novel expands the list with other familiar items. Related to the major themes of responsibility and the evasion of it, there are others: the need for Charity and the insufficiency of charity (the social services); the desire for independence and the need for community; the desire for privacy and the need to share; the general dislike of the old; and the seeming lack of options and hope for the elderly. In her treatment of these complex subjects, Pym raises large questions: Who is my neighbor? What is the responsibility of one human being to another? Who is responsible for someone who cannot be responsible for himself?

Pym gives us the key to the novel's moral perspective both in Edwin's allusion to the parable of the Good Samaritan and in the rueful question Father Gellibrand asks himself when he recognizes his reluctance to visit Marcia:

> "Who is my neighbour?" Father G. mused, as he and Edwin came to the road where Marcia lived. "Surely one has preached often enough on that text? Perhaps that's where we go wrong—obviously it *is*—when my reaction to your suggestion is that the person in question isn't in my parish." (162)

In the Bible, the lawyer who asks what he must do to be saved is referred to the Law he already knows: he must love God, and love his neighbor as himself. When he asks the question Gellibrand repeats, Jesus answers with the parable of the Samaritan. Though contemporary London is very far removed from biblical times and places, it is the locale of several modern versions of the parable. There is, first, Letty's experience on the train platform when she sees the woman (who reminds her of an old friend) slumped over, apparently not well. Letty has to force herself to look, and then wonders if she ought to help. While she hesitates, a young woman speaks softly to the bent figure and is answered by a roaring "Fuck off!" Letty sees the girl, "braver" than she was, move away with "dignity." Another time, Marcia hears an ambulance bell and joins the circle standing around a man lying on the sidewalk. She watches the ambulance attendants restrain him as he tries to get up and is happy to see them taking him away. She is pleased because she sees a symbol of her own Samaritan in action.

It would not occur to Marcia to describe the medical establishment in that term because she is not a churchgoer, but she has experienced in her illness a personal version of the parable. She was ill and the medical people acted to help her, almost in spite of herself. Marcia remembers the experience as if all volition, all responsibility, had been taken out of her hands. Despite her determination never to submit to surgery, "when it came to the point there was no question of resistance," and Mr. Strong performed the mastectomy. She dislikes it when people want to discuss "sacred matters"— details about Mr. Strong—with her, but every memory Marcia has of her stay in the hospital is positive and cherished. The Asian orderly who called her "dear," the lady who brought her tea (whose name she still remembers), and all the rest were there to care for her. Without asking if she wanted it, they assumed she needed their help and gave it, and Marcia basked in their attentions and in Mr. Strong's concern for her well-being. It is little wonder that she worships him as the central figure of her universe:

> If the surgeon was God, the chaplains were his ministers, a little lower than the housemen. The good-looking young Roman Catholic had come first, saying . . . how being in hospital, unpleasant though it was in many ways, could sometimes prove to be a blessing in disguise. (19)

It was certainly a blessing for Marcia, who found God-on-earth in her surgeon and a religion based not on faith, but on experience: she was sick and they cared for her. Unfortunately, her most serious illness is not physical, and she is not in her haven. Her story is a bizarre and horrifying version of the parable in a world where physical ailments and medical ministrations are the only socially acceptable forms of need and responsive care.

By the time we meet Marcia, already she has nothing to give or receive, having fallen among the most successful of thieves. Time and death have stripped her of her family, her mother, and Snowy, her cat. She still misses Snowy and keeps a "relic," a dried-up fur ball. Her loneliness, unrecognized by herself, is most apparent in her effort to locate his grave, to find his bones in her overgrown garden. She has no relatives except a cousin whom she has not seen in some forty years, and no interest that she acknowledges in anyone, except Mr. Strong, her distant god. The interest she once had in Norman has faded, the result of her inability to satisfy her curiosity by speaking to him and of his deliberate avoidance of her. Though her coworker can still elicit a miniscule response from her, Marcia is entirely alone.

Her age as well as her solitude isolates her. Retirement means that her daily contact with others, however restrained and superficial, will be over, and that she will be stranded by a physical isolation to match her emotional condition. Her old neighbors have been replaced by a young couple who would prefer others like themselves next door and who share, despite their little efforts with Marcia, the generally negative attitudes toward the elderly. When Priscilla chats with Janice Brabner, they express a subdued exasperation toward Marcia and all troublesome old people. Father Gellibrand, from whom we might hope for a better attitude, draws away from Letty when Edwin refers to her as "a senior citizen," not much caring "for the aged, the elderly, or just 'old people,' whatever you liked to call them." With terrible irony, Pym shows us that the quartet, in their sixties, have accepted the general outlook. Letty feels it is "unfair" of Edwin so to categorize her when she has so little gray in her hair, and Norman once advises against getting "landed with an elderly person." In one way or another, they unthinkingly conspire with the public relegation of the old to a life of diminishment. Old people do not need much to eat, do not need vacations (and certainly not trips to Spain, as Edwin's daughter concludes)—old people do not need any number of things. Marcia, remarking to her officemates that "when you're older you don't really need holidays," and eating less and less all the time, would seem to agree with her society's prescription for the aged.

She is already slipping away when the novel opens, a victim of the defensive attitudes for the self and toward others, all of which she shares with her officemates. One of their major preoccupations is privacy, keeping others at arm's length. Pym's title suggests that Marcia, Letty, Norman, and Edwin are a natural group, whose similarities the latter enumerates: "Four people on the verge of retirement, each one of us living alone, and without any close relative near—that's us." In the office, they are two couples linked by proximity and natural affinity—but in the most distant, restrained manner imaginable. Edwin offers Letty his bag of jelly babies after lunch in "a ritual gesture," though he knows she will refuse, and Marcia makes instant coffee for Norman and herself since it is cheaper to buy and share the larger can. Edwin and Letty are more optimistic and positive than their friends. Edwin, by structuring his life around the Church and the Church calendar, provides himself with a hobby and activity; Letty, with her interest in her appearance and her guarded interest in the world around her, suggests that she still wishes to relate to others. Marcia and Norman are the more negative, pessimistic pair. Norman is filled with the bitter anger of deprivation and despair against anyone and anything that reminds him of the emptiness of his own life. Marcia's withdrawal is the stage that follows despair. From time to time, Norman and Marcia exasperate the other two because they will not (or cannot) do anything to help themselves.

Marcia feels she is an "incomplete" woman because of her mastectomy, but Letty feels the same about herself. Something must be missing in her, she continually accuses herself, that she could not find love and make the family she thinks would have saved her from her present loneliness. She is wrong to think a family necessarily means protection from the fears of a lonely old age: Edwin's wife died and his daughter and her family are not a significant part of his everyday life; Mrs. Pope, with her prominent photograph of Mr. Pope, apparently has no one except the friends she has acquired by her years in the Church and the lodger she decides to take in. Letty continually berates herself for her "failure" and does not see that Norman, Edwin, and Marcia are also "incomplete": they cannot reach out to others any more than she can for friendship or companionship, let alone for affection or love. The four people working together day after day do not consider themselves "friends," do not socialize outside of the office, and have never been at each other's homes. These men and women cannot acknowledge their status as a small community created by proximity, familiarity, and shared human needs.

The desire for privacy implied by the quartet's strict separation of their working and their "personal" lives comes to seem in the course of the novel a defensive combination of pride and shame at being seen as, or considered to be, remotely needy in any way. Such defenses may spring from dignity and pride, but also from the underlying awareness that most people are repelled by neediness in any form. Letty, almost defeated by the lonely unstructured days of retirement, yet tells the others that she fills her time " 'quite pleasantly.' She must never give the slightest hint of loneliness or boredom, the sense of time hanging heavy." Everyone knows, as Marcia says, that "a woman can always find plenty to occupy her time," and Letty considers her problem another unique personal failure. Norman, whose poverty relative to Edwin shames him, accepts the Christmas invitation of Ken, his widowed brother-in-law, and his new fiancée almost as a favor to them, to help them eat their turkey. Later, the possibility of sharing Edwin's house zips through his mind like a hare pursued by hounds. Edwin would not dream of telling his coworkers that spending Christmas with his daughter's family was unenjoyable. Even Marcia, so remote from normal social considerations, competently uses the standard defensive phrases:

> I go out to work and my evenings are fully occupied. (30)

> When they asked how she had spent her leave she was evasive, only saying that the weather had been good and she'd had a nice break, which was what people always said. (51)

> There's a young woman who comes round to see me sometimes—seems to think I need help. . . . It's the other way round, if you ask me. (69)

> We who work in offices do value our leisure time, so we don't need to make elaborate plans. (87)

Their fierce protection of privacy means that Edwin, Letty, Norman, and Marcia hide their needs, precluding even the remote possibility that someone might help.

Next to privacy, the quartet believes in the desirability of not getting involved. We mentioned Letty's hesitation when she sees the woman on the train platform and Norman's caution to her about living with Mrs. Pope, about getting "landed with an elderly person and all *that* entails." In this respect, Marcia is different from the others mainly in the degree of her uninvolvement. She resents people who try to chat with her even casually, on the bus or at the doctors' offices. When Norman, focusing as usual on catastrophe, brings up the threat of hypothermia, she does not share the information she has literally at her fingertips about the heat allowances for elderly people. The "alien" milk bottle she discovers in her tidy hoard and finally identifies as belonging to Letty bothers her immensely as a worrisome intrusion of the other woman into her life—it involves her with Letty.

Clearly, involvement has the potential of discovering need and, as such, of implying responsibility on the part of the one who sees it. The discomfort of such an eventuality is apparent in Norman's reaction, while visiting at the hospital, to Ken's remark that the tea he was served is too strong: "He hadn't come here to be involved in this sort of thing," Norman thinks angrily, feeling that some vague demand has been made, unfairly and unreasonably, of him. Edwin is "sometimes haunted" by an image of Norman in a small bedsitter while he lives in a house, but would not dream of actually referring to the other man's living arrangements. However, the ostriches are unable to ignore the crisis of one of their kind when Letty tells them she must move away from Mr. Olatunde and his "disturbing" kind of Nigerian Christianity. Marcia cannot bring herself to enter the discussion, fearing

> that she might have to offer Letty a room in her house. After all, Letty had always been kind to her; she had once offered to make her a cup of tea before going home, and though the offer had not been accepted it had not been forgotten. But this did not mean that Marcia was under any obligation to provide accommodation for Letty in her retirement. For of course it would be impossible. . . . the difficulties were insuperable.

> Women alone had to make their own way in the world and no
> doubt Letty already knew this. (59–60)

No one here wants claims made on their time, energy, space, or emotions—and to insure their own independence from the demands of responsibility, they insist on the independence of others. Only Edwin, whose sex protects him from the possibility of having to offer Letty a room, helps her by putting her in touch with Mrs. Pope.

In stressing Marcia's participation in the general, alienating attitudes toward privacy, responsibility, and independence, I am not suggesting a direct cause-and-effect relationship between her failures to connect and the others' failures toward her; the people around her do not treat her as they do *because* of the way she treats them—her attitudes are typical. Letty and Edwin are more self-helping than the other two, but have the same problems. They feel an urge, more often than Marcia and Norman, to help others, but do not often act on these little twinges. What happens to Marcia could have happened to any one of the others while the other three stood by, at a safe distance and with eyes carefully averted.

Before Marcia retires, the others refuse to acknowledge that something seems to be wrong with her. Their feeling is that her mastectomy "made her more peculiar than she had been already." Letty, whose loneliness is acute and who yearns to matter to someone, has an insight that results in the gesture of kindness Marcia later remembers: "Outside, the pigeons on the roof were picking at each other, presumably removing insects. Perhaps this is all that we as human beings can do for each other." But when Marcia refuses her "unsentimental tenderness . . . expressed in small gestures of solicitude," Letty does not consider her condition again. Edwin, finding himself on the street where Marcia lives, leaves speedily, assuming that she would be as embarrassed and dismayed as he at "any kind of encounter." Besides, he tells himself, if anyone ought to visit her, it should be Norman. Norman, admiring his used satin dressing gown, speculates about the kinds Edwin and Letty might wear, but does not like to think about Marcia's and finds his thoughts rapidly "sheering away from her." While she is still working, her coworkers, as if by common consent, will not acknowledge her condition.

Later, however, when a touch of conscience makes Edwin arrange a lunch date with the retired women, Marcia's state cannot be ignored. She decides to go only because it will be an opportunity to return Letty's milk bottle, and startles them by her "strange appearance," her thinness, her odd combination of clothes, and her partly undyed hair. She refuses to be cajoled into eating much of anything and barely participates in the conversation. When Edwin asks what she has been doing, her answer is quick: "That's my business." She is in a hurry to leave and seems to soften only for a moment when Norman speaks to her. Pym leaves us in no doubt that Marcia's old coworkers understand she is in trouble:

> Norman thought, poor old girl, obviously going round the bend. Letty, as a clothes-conscious woman, was appalled—that anyone could get to the stage of caring so little about her appearance, of not even noticing how she looked, made her profoundly uneasy and almost conscience-stricken, as if *she* ought to have done something more about Marcia in her retirement. (130)

But Letty feels she is off the hook, having already extended an ignored invitation to lunch. When Marcia returns her milk bottle with embarrassingly loud explanations, she resolutely ignores the significance of the bizarre action and does not pursue the connection she senses between this incident and the one of the woman on the underground platform. The men do slightly better in the situation calling for a Good Samaritan. Norman speaks bluntly to Marcia at the restaurant about her thinness and mentions anorexia. Though he and Edwin reassure themselves that they need do nothing since "people [like the doctor and the social worker] do seem to be keeping an eye on her," Norman eventually goes to Marcia's house. After catching a glimpse of her from across the street, he actually crosses it (as Edwin can never bring himself to do) but is accosted while he hesitates by Janice Brabner. He might have done something grand had he not been challenged as a possible elderly malefactor, but as it is, he flees and is able to reassure himself and the slightly guilty Edwin that someone is indeed keeping an eye on Marcia.

Since Marcia's small circle, those who, as Edwin thinks, "might be just the people to be in a position to help her or at least to offer help," fails her, she is entirely in the hands of the professional Good Samaritans. Actually, it is more accurate to say she is in their field of vision. The phrase "keeping an eye on" is repeated often enough, while Marcia's condition deteriorates, to underscore its meaninglessness. The disembodied eyes of the Church, the medical establishment, and the social services all flick over her. The local church extends an invitation for a coach trip, "but she didn't seem to want to go and of course they couldn't force her." When Marcia goes to Mr. Strong's clinic for a checkup, the inexperienced intern tells her she should eat more and remarks that "perhaps somebody should keep an eye on" her, so she is given an appointment for a future date. She is eyed again when she goes without an appointment to a public clinic where another doctor tells her she should eat more, but he considers that things are "out of his hands" since Mr. Strong's "boys" will be taking a look at her in the future. In spite of Marcia's faith, this minister of her cult fails to notice that she is starving herself. He does nothing, although as she talks to him incoherently he is "given a decided impression that all was not quite as it should be."

Marcia's starvation and her descent into mental imbalance are punctuated by visits from Janice Brabner, a volunteer social worker at the community center. Though she is sometimes tactless, Janice's biggest problems are Marcia's entirely unreceptive attitude, her own lack of common sense, and her dislike for a woman who is not responsive and grateful for her efforts. She is exasperated by Marcia as an unrewarding type: "People like that don't seem to *want* to be helped," she laments. Janice believes, as a matter of course and despite what "an older and more experienced colleague" says, that one cannot force people to take help. Still, she continues to drop by, fully respecting Marcia's privacy and independence while "keeping an eye on" her. Seeing the dirt in Marcia's unkempt house, Janice decides she must not interfere—"Some people didn't like doing housework, anyway."

Her attitude is like Priscilla's when she sees her neighbor trying to dig up something in her overgrown garden with a spade: "one couldn't bully the elderly, their independence was their last remaining treasure and must be respected." Janice knows, from Nigel and Priscilla, about Marcia's collection of milk bottles. But even this does not dampen her enthusiasm for Marcia's privacy and independence:

> It seemed a curiously dotty occupation, but harmless enough—just the kind of thing Marcia would spend her time doing, but no more to be condemned than other people's preoccupation with collecting matchboxes or cigarette cards. One *must* respect people as individuals—her acquaintance with Marcia had taught Janice that, if nothing else. (160)

At Marcia's crisis, Janice is joined by Edwin and Father Gellibrand, coming to pay their first call on the woman who has been nagging her coworker's conscience for so long. Neither of the men is happy about doing his duty, though Gellibrand rebukes himself, a few moments before Janice tells them of Marcia's collapse, with the question of "Who is my neighbour?"

Marcia is taken away by the only Samaritans she accepts, whose appearance she has anticipated with a stash of new nightgowns. "Somebody loves you, don't they," a nurse coos at her as she delivers a bouquet of flowers from Edwin, Letty, and Norman. The woman in the next bed marvels when two more bouquets arrive for Marcia, who "looked the kind of person who wouldn't get any." The gravity of her illness, because it unquestionably makes Marcia the responsibility of the hospital, enables her former coworkers to acknowledge relationship with her. Norman, who is more affected than the others, tells Edwin that he "always thinks of her at coffee time" and refers, with the flippancy he uses to disguise emotion, to his "romantic memories." Letty does not permit Mrs. Pope to suggest that she hardly knows Marcia, thinking to herself that they were linked by "a special kind of tie—all the dull routine, the petty grumbles and the shared irritation of the men." Stopping at the hospital, Edwin is asked about Marcia's next of kin and reports with some embarrassment to Norman: "I had to give myself. . . . I said I was her next of kin."

Marcia's regrets at not having confronted Norman when she saw him looking at her, at her house, from across the road, and her puzzlement over why nothing developed from her earlier interest in him, strongly suggest her disappointment with Norman and with herself. Neither of them had the will to move toward the other, and the reason for this baffles Marcia, who has just remembered, before thinking of Norman, Nigel's offer to cut her grass: "she preferred it that way; it kept people out." Her confusion gives way to concern over Mr. Strong's frown looming over her, but at the last minute, her smile seems to elicit a response.

When Marcia dies, the first order of business is denial of responsibility. The chaplain who talks to Edwin, expecting a grieving relative, is pleased to find "just a 'friend'" with an interesting attitude: "Rather surprisingly, he held the view that there was nothing to reproach oneself with for not having been able to prevent death when, for the Christian, it was so much to be desired." In spite of this view, Edwin seems to feel that "the social worker and the neighbour [who] put in an appearance" at the funeral failed in their responsibility. Janice, on the other hand, feels no guilt and resents the "friends" who might have visited Marcia but never did. Pym's allusions to the parable of the Good Samaritan implicate all of them. The man waylaid, beaten by thieves, and left to die on the road is in no condition to call for the help he needs, which makes it easier for the priest and the Levite to pass by on the other side. When the Good Samaritan comes along, he does not inquire whether the dying man wants his help. He does not worry, either, about violating that man's privacy and independence: he sees, feels compassion, and takes responsibility for the man who cannot take responsibility for himself. Marcia, according to Janice, "might be said to have fallen through the net," and no wonder—all those eyes being kept on her, when what she needed was a hand or even a supporting arm.

The sense of waste so powerfully evoked by Marcia's death is almost redeemed by her legacies to her friends, chief of which is the relationship into which they are thrown. Seeing Edwin's house for the first time, Letty realizes that "Death has done this." At first she feels that Marcia's death means she is completely alone, but then realizes that she and the men are "very much alive." No one has any piercing insights, but Marcia's death creates new situations that must elicit new responses to each other. Edwin sees Norman's emotion at the lunch following the service and plans to invite him for a meal in order to give him the opportunity to talk about Marcia. Having noticed that Letty seems lonely, he calls her on the telephone, though he does not reach her. Norman, needing someone to help sort Marcia's clothes, turns to Letty because "it would be better than having a stranger." Left Marcia's house and so given the freedom and power to choose what he wants for himself, Norman first chooses generosity. He is the host who shares Marcia's stored cans of food and drinks the bottle of sherry with his newfound little community of friends. Though it is hopeful, this secular communion is not perfect. Edwin is obscurely distressed by Letty. She is enjoying her power to decide for herself where she wants to live and the knowledge that her decision matters and will make a substantial difference to Marjorie and Mrs. Pope. On a subconscious level, Edwin realizes he might have to feel a friend's responsibility for her if she stays in London—and the unspoken possibility does not fill him with unqualified delight. But Letty offers the men the more immediate prospect of a day in the country with her and Marjorie. A new, harmonious quartet might be too much to hope for, but Pym ends the novel with Letty's realization "that life still held infinite possibilities for change."

Reading *Quartet in Autumn*, we move continually between indignation and recognition. Pym reminds us of the Christian imperative and at the same time of the many attitudes and assumptions with which we have qualified it or made it easy to ignore. Like Leonora Eyre, Marcia Ivory is an extreme case. But in Letty, Edwin, Norman, and the other characters, Pym insists that we recognize the ordinary defenses we all employ to keep from seeing in others or exposing in ourselves the emotional needs that might, at least, unite us. We hear the catchphrases like concrete blocks behind which we guard our *privacy* and *independence*, words beyond criticism, nearly sacred, that too often mean solitude and irresponsibility. Though Edwin, who remembers Fathers Thames and Bode (*GB*), is a regular churchgoer, and though the novel's moral perspective is indicated by biblical allusions, Pym is not writing about love in the exclusively Christian context. Christianity has institutionalized the concept of loving one's neighbor, but the idea of a compassionate benevolence toward others is familiar to all. The author calls our attention to "just the ordinary responsibility of one human being towards another," as Letty says, a responsibility that assumes relationship and compels assistance to those in need. "All those years wasted, looking for love," Letty thinks at a particularly low point. She means romantic love and laments in its lack the absence of relationship, which she believes would have kept her from emotional isolation. But romantic love, Pym suggests in *Quartet in Autumn*, is not by any means the sole form of redemptive relationship.

A Few Green Leaves

In *A Few Green Leaves*, Pym returns to the comic perspective and to some of her favorite themes. Observation versus participation, unsuitable attachments, the need for love and relationship, options for emotional fulfillment, independence and the need for community—all of these are touched upon, in the context of the search for identity by a contemporary woman living in an outpost of our modern world. Some darker threads from *Quartet in Autumn*, having been turned just so, add their rich depth to this essentially cheerful tapestry: Pym deals with the need for faith in our largely secular world, attitudes toward the aged, and death, achieving resonance without grimness in her depiction of contemporary life. Her deliberate presentation of Emma Howick as a modern woman trying to find meaning in her life and surroundings, of Tom as a man preoccupied with the past, and of the general assumption of an enlightened or different "present" combine to pose important questions: What is constant in a world of change? What has the past to offer aggressively modern people?

The West Oxfordshire village where Emma Howick comes to stay in her mother's cottage might seem, with its manor house and picturesque cottages, a throwback to earlier days. In spite of its size and small-town atmosphere, however, it is contemporary. Most of the townswomen work, there is a general awareness that the people cannot (perhaps even *should* not) be treated as if the old class distinctions applied, and the social services are very much a part of the land-scape, with the result, according to one character, that all are "flattened out into a kind of uniform dullness these days— something to do with the welfare state and the rise of the consumer society." Without looking closely, it is sometimes difficult to tell a young man from a young woman, jeans and t-shirt being the uniform that unisexes swains and maidens. A food critic holds forth on spaghetti, certain fish sauces, and the proper slicing of cucumber. People eat convenience foods and almost everyone watches television, on which it is not unusual to see women participating as experts in panel discussions. This community may be small, but it is entirely today.

Perhaps the most persuasive evidence for the modernity of the village is the general attitude toward medicine. Like Marcia Ivory, most of the villagers believe fervently in the medical sciences, and for them the doctors' office is the new sanctuary:

> Monday was always a busy day at the surgery . . . . "They"— the patients—had not on the whole been to church the previous day, but they atoned for this by a devout attendance at the place where they expected not so much to worship, though this did come into it for a few, as to receive advice and consolation. You might *talk* to the rector, some would admit doubtfully, but he couldn't give you a prescription. There was nothing in churchgoing to equal that triumphant moment when you came out of the surgery clutching the ritual scrap of paper. (13)

Pym's diction points to the villagers' need for faith, their need for something or someone to believe in and turn to for help in their troubles. Medicine is obviously the new religion of many considering the number of people who consult Martin Shrubsole and Luke Gellibrand (brother of Edwin's Father Gellibrand) for aches and pains that cannot be palpated or even located in the body. Perhaps the most surprising of these patients is Daphne Dagnall, whose complaint is the modern catchall, depression—a grievous dislike for the damp village when she would rather be in sunny Greece. Daphne is as delighted with the opportunity to talk over her situation with Dr. Shrubsole as with the prescription he gives her. She is proud to report that he asked if she wanted tranquilizers, but when her brother asks politely about her answer, she snubs him. The confidentiality between doctor and patient, she says, is inviolable, "like the confessional." The new faith is not fazed, either, by intangible ailments that tranquilizers or placebos cannot alleviate. Martin Shrubsole is always ready to recommend "psychiatric help."

Martin and Avice, his wife and a former social worker, represent everything that is repellent in our savvy, psychologically slick outlook. Avice is one of those bossy, opinionated women who look on others with the smug pity of the know-it-all for the less progressive or well-informed. She is a take-charge woman in any situation that tries her patience or seems (to her) to call for her firm hand. Manipulation is her style. Since she covets Tom's large rectory, for instance, she invites him to dinner in order to plant the idea that he might move into a small cottage.

Martin is a gerontologist, and Pym describes him as he edges away from Daphne's emotional response to some flowers:

> Although he was a kind man and keenly interested in the elderly and those in late middle age, his interest was detached and clinical. He enjoyed taking blood pressures . . . but was disinclined to enter into other aspects of their lives. He felt that the drugs prescribed to control high blood pressure should also damp down emotional excesses and those fires of youth that could still—regrettably—burn in the dried-up hearts of those approaching old age. (5)

Martin's is the enlightened attitude about old people: exercise, a proper diet, and some interest more intellectual than watching television are all to be encouraged. Unfortunately, the fairly young doctor does not really like the elderly and certainly cannot see his mother-in-law or his patients as his equals in intellect or maturity. He speaks to Magdalen about the hunger lunch with the kind of overbright enthusiasm we reserve for discussions with children about liver or okra. Ordinary chat with her seems a duty to him, since such conversation, "though no doubt therapeutic for her, was so often a waste of time for him." Even Dr. Gellibrand, who is old himself, does not like to treat the elderly, preferring young mothers who represent "the whole idea of life burgeoning and going on" to reminders of his own mortality. Still, most of the older people in the novel are relatively fortunate. Avice and Martin feel crowded in their house by the presence of Magdalen, who knows her daughter uses her as a built-in babysitter—but despite these annoying drawbacks, she is given a home and considers herself lucky to have it. The legendary Miss Vereker is held in "superstitious veneration" by the nephew she lives with and feels, in her seventies, that she has "entered yet another sacred category, that of 'the aged.'" The Misses Lee and Grundy live together, and only Miss Lickerish, the "elderly village eccentric," seems to have no relatives or friends to look after her. Since her numerous relatives do not include her in their circle, she makes her own, occasionally attending social functions in the village and looking after a family of "her cats and the hedgehogs, and once even a toad."

Perhaps a keen interest in the past is to be expected of the many older people in the village. In her many references to Miss Vereker, Miss Lee continually conjures up a past she remembers as more satisfactory and gracious than the present. It sounds like another world—a time of governesses, manor houses with private chapels, and paternalistic treats for the villagers. Some details provided by Dr. Gellibrand hint at a secret unknown to Miss Vereker's friends: "the last governess" was "quite a young woman in those days," he tells Tom, who liked to hang out in the family's mausoleum—a place he still frequents and to which he has one of the two keys. Could it be an old-fashioned story of an unsuitable attachment and renunciation that Dr. Gellibrand remembers among the marble heads and limbs? Miss Vereker represents the past, so often spoken of that her return to the village to see old friends (and visit the mausoleum) "before she died" is a symbolic action elucidating other aspects of the novel. By coming, she brings the past into the present—a pattern reflected in the experiences of Emma and Tom. But her awareness of impending death suggests that inevitably something is passing away, perhaps the old-fashioned styles of romance and femininity she represents.

Tom Dagnall is as enamored of the past as Miss Lee, though he looks back to previous centuries, especially the seventeenth. His hero is Anthony à Wood, the late seventeenth-century diarist. As the head and chief mover of the local history society, Tom looks continually for signs of the past in the present and tries to preserve such signs by putting volunteers to work copying names and dates from gravestones. His greatest desire is to find the deserted medieval village. The D.M.V., as everyone calls it, would be simply a pile of stones, so it is hard to understand what particular interest or satisfaction its location could possibly give a man who is not an archaeologist or even a historian but a country rector. Tom's preoccupation with history indicates his uncertainty about the present role of the Church and his detached attitude as an observer; it also reflects his sense of personal entrapment in the amber of the past. As a rector in a largely secularized society, Tom feels like the old man caught in the new world. The new man, whose metamorphosis seems a subtle comment on Tom's adherence to an outmoded role, is Adam Prince. Adam's evolution from Anglican priest to food critic, a guru in the cult of consumerism, seems to mock Tom as a figure of the past.

Tom's adoption of the role of historian turns him into a detached observer of the world around him—he is so preoccupied with the invisible world that was, once upon a time, that he does not see the one before him. His fascination with history is an evasion, a strategy for displacing his concern about his relevance in the present time. He searches for the D.M.V. because he cannot deal with the real village in which he lives; he assumes the neutral role of historian because he is unable to relate to people comfortably as a priest. Needing to discover the continuity of his ancient faith in the contemporary situation, Tom looks for physical evidence of the past in his surroundings. At one point, his search for personal significance leads him to emulate his hero: he figures he can be an observer for the future and starts a diary, recording the banal details of his life in the hope that they might be of interest to historians of the next century. It is an interesting feat, making a mental leap into the next century in order to see himself as a figure of the past. Tom's attachment to history simultaneously suggests his fears that Christianity is a thing of the past and reminds us that his responsibility as a priest is the successful "mingling of past and present."

In his personal life, Tom is imprisoned in the past. Duty, as Ogden Nash wrote, does not have "the visage of a sweetie or a cutie," and for Tom it has Daphne's dour puss. Feeling it was her responsibility to "make a home for him" when Laura, his wife, died, she unthinkingly helped this passive man to stall in the role of widower, never deciding what he actually wanted or making a new life for himself. In fact, he regressed into his past life as the baby brother of a bossy elder sister. Pym does not present this arrangement as a satisfactory option for the emotional well-being of either. Daphne bristles around Tom with all the hostility of a disgruntled teen-ager forced to babysit an irksome brat. She would rather be in Greece, possibly accompanied by a nice dog. Tom's loneliness and sense of uselessness are exacerbated by her disdain for everything he does or in which he takes an interest. He is made to feel he is in the way, especially when his sister and Mrs. Dyer are cleaning. Tom is a rector who feels superfluous even in the rectory.

Since the only excellent women in the village are the elderly Misses Lee and Grundy, Tom is not the desirable clerical object of any maidenly dreams. (It cannot be doubted that Miss Lee, especially, would have been the right type: for her vacation, she goes to the Anchorage, the place advertised to Dulcie Mainwaring [NFR] as having a "bright Christian atmosphere.") Just as Tom has ignored his need for love, Cupid seems disposed to ignore this muddled parson-historian—certainly, Emma is not the type to build romantic fantasies around a clergyman. In fact, as a modern woman, she is not the type to nurture romantic fantasies at all. Like Tom, she does not feel or recognize the need for love. In this sophistication, she believes she is unlike her mother, whose studies in the Victorian novel suggest to Emma an old-fashioned perspective on women vis-à-vis men. An anthropologist, Emma has come to the village "to detach herself from the harsh realities of her field notes and perhaps even find inspiration for a new and different study." Unlike the anthropologists of an earlier day, people like Everard Bone or Helena Napier, Emma has not gone to Africa. The "field" she observes with detachment is the English community, of which the Oxfordshire village she lives in is an example.

Emma's modernity does not consist merely of her having a profession. Esther Clovis was "a formidable female power in the anthropological world" of Emma's youth, and her death is marked by a memorial service attended by prominent scholars like Digby Fox (accompanied by Deirdre), Dr. Apfelbaum, Gertrude Lydgate, and Father Gemini. Beatrix Howick, Emma's mother, is a tutor of English literature at a women's college. Since she named her daughter for Jane Austen's character, we are especially aware of Emma as a version of the contemporary heroine in her assumptions, attitudes, and mores. Naturally, she assumes her independence and her ability to make her own fulfilling life; initially, she does not evince or acknowledge dissatisfaction with her single state. There is no question of her sitting around thinking that she wants a man or that she wants to be married.

However, though Emma has come to the village as a detached observer, and though her need for relationship is unacknowledged, her actions reveal a desire for connectedness, or "human contact," as some of the characters say. During her first weekend in the village, "she had been planning to observe the inhabitants" from behind her curtains, but cannot "resist the temptation" to join the group taking the annual walk in the woods. The same evening, she sees Graham Pettifer on a television panel discussion and writes immediately, inviting him (and perhaps his wife) to drop by. When she walks by the busy surgery on the following day,

> she was tempted to join in what seemed like an enjoyable occasion from which she was being excluded. But remembering her role as an anthropologist and observer—the necessity of being on the outside looking in—she crept away, meditating on what she had observed. There was obviously material for a note here. (20)

Emma may perceive her interest in others and her wish to be around them as doing her work, but anyone who sees people sitting in the doctors' waiting room as an attractive party is lonely. The image with which she remembers her scholarly role has an almost Dickensian pathos: the urchin-anthropologist presses her nose to the cold glass, looking at the merry feast that is not, alas, for the likes of her. Notwithstanding Emma's self-sufficiency and seeming contentment with her life, an underlying sense of emotional isolation and deprivation motivates her behavior.

Like Tom, Emma seeks meaning in her surroundings. As she goes around observing, titles for possible scholarly papers occur to her: "Some Observations on the Social Patterns of a West Oxfordshire Village," "The Role of Women in a West Oxfordshire Community," and "Funeral Customs in a Rural Community." Her invitation to Graham Pettifer suggests that she is also looking for some kind of meaning in her life. Though Emma knows he is married now and that he might, if he comes, bring his wife (one of her mother's former students), her letter is a reaching out, an impulse to establish some kind of connection between her present and her former life, in which she was a woman involved with Graham rather than a detached anthropologist. When she hears the moderator of the television show call him by name,

> she realised that this was Graham Pettifer, a man with whom she had once had a brief love affair. To say that he had been her "lover" was altogether too grand a way to describe what their association had been; perhaps even "love affair" was not strictly accurate, for there had not been all that much love about it, no more than proximity and a mild affection. (11)

Emma's appraisal of her relationship with Graham is determinedly analytical. There is about it the cool matter-of-factness that is the modern antidote to sentimentalizing or exaggerating the emotional significance of sex. But her ambivalence about who she is and what she wants for herself is apparent: she simultaneously denies the importance of her past and summons it into the present.

When Graham arrives alone and with news of his separation from Claudia, Emma has no thought whatever of his being "unsuitable" by virtue of being still married. (It is impossible not to think of the guilt Belinda Bede and Mildred Lathbury felt for their chaste interests in married men—times have changed and heroines with them.) She launches into a bad replay of the past. At least, we can hope it is a bad replay: her new relationship with Graham is awkward, half-hearted, especially on his part, and affectionate only in theory. Seeing her for the first time in several years, he remarks to himself on her unattractiveness, especially on her having "pitifully little 'bosom-wise.'" He grants their past association even less significance than Emma does and assumes complacently that she was "anxious" to see him again. Her lack of beauty and breasts does not prevent him from using her; he is willing that she should listen to his story about Claudia, and later, when he decides to move into the cottage in the woods, that she should help him with the practical details of setting up house, cook for him, keep him company (when he is not busy), and generally make him comfortable indoors and out:

> "Do people pass along this way? Will anybody see us?" He started to kiss and fondle her in a rather abstracted way. Emma found herself remembering Miss Lickerish and the goings-on in the ruined cottage during the war. "I hope we should have some warning," she said, "see them coming through the trees."
> "This is rather pleasant, isn't it?" he said. "I feel I deserve a break from my work," he added, as if being with her could be no more than that. (148)

It is not so pleasant that the wary Graham decides to repeat the experience. Casual sex is fine when it fits his work schedule, but he fears that Emma will assume a relationship he does not really want. While he is carefully meting out a safe degree of lukewarm attention to her, she is waiting for a repetition of their "amorous dalliance on the grass." This phrase, which Emma uses only to herself, suggests a desire for romance beneath her irony.

The reappearance of Graham brings into focus both Beatrix's dissatisfactions with her daughter and some contemporary attitudes about the relationship between men and women. Beatrix believes that all women should marry or have some kind of "important" relationship with a man. Her own experience suggests that this relationship need not be permanent or even very lengthy: she married, had a daughter, lost her husband in the war, and then was able to turn her attention, "with a clear conscience," to her studies. In addition to her own experience, she knows too many spinsters like Isobel Mound, Flavia Grundy, and Olive Lee not to know that unmarried women can lead fulfilled, satisfying, and useful lives. What Beatrix understands is missing in her daughter, which she assumes a serious relationship with a man would evoke, is emotional commitment, the experience of giving herself to someone or something.

Since her work, despite its emphasis on "The Significance of" this or that, does not mean much to her, she looks for meaning in the relationship with Graham. She longs for a clear story line that will help her define her particular role and significance in the scheme of things: "There are only a few twists to the man-woman story. For instance, it would be more satisfactory if Graham could . . . indicate something of his feelings, even. That might help her to clarify her own, for she was not sure whether she wanted him or not." Her encounters with Claudia leave her feeling disappointed because Graham's wife is so friendly. Claudia has no curiosity about the nature of Emma's relationship with her husband, nor does Graham have any interest in Emma's encounters with his wife. Clearly, Emma does have a story in mind despite her vagueness about it, but the other key characters refuse steadfastly to see that there is a "situation existing between the three of them." Something is lacking in a story in which the wife sincerely asks the other woman to keep an eye on the husband.

Even after the wretched man is gone, Emma searches for evidence that her involvement with him meant something. She finds an anthology of seventeenth-century poetry in his vacated cottage, but is disappointed when it opens to Crashaw's "Upon Two Green Apricots Sent to Cowley by Sir Crashaw." Eventually she learns that it belongs to Tom and that Graham had borrowed it to look up an allusion in a letter from Claudia. The scene on the Christmas card she gets from him she considers an allusion to his stay at the cottage, until she tells herself that men are not "subtle in *that* way" and is reminded by her mother that Claudia probably chose it. Earlier, when Avice tried to draw her out, she "fiercely" denied that she had expected anything of Graham. To Beatrix, she denies that she did much of anything for him. But to Martin, after Graham left, she suggested that a rash on her hands might be evidence of "stress," and she thought of inviting Tom to dinner in revealing terms: "After all, they were two lonely people now, and as such should get to-gether." Emma had hoped that the relationship with Graham would develop in some way that would be gratifying to her-self and is disappointed when it does not happen.

However, the unsatisfactory relationship is not a total loss. Graham brings the past into the present for Emma—it was a case, as Tom remarks, of her "first love reappearing." The importance of the interlude had nothing to do with the iden-tity of the lover but everything to do with Emma's: by her invitation, she was trying to recover not Graham but herself as a loving woman— and in that sense the episode was a success. The combination of her experience and Beatrix's probing contribute to Emma's understanding of what she wants, an insight she reaches at the Christmas midnight ser-vice at Tom's church:

> Emma, sitting between her mother and Isobel, found herself wishing that she had a man with her, though the idea of the man being Graham did not appeal to her. Some nebulous, comfortable—even handsome—figure suggested itself, which made her realise that even the most cynical and sophisticated woman is not, at times, altogether out of sympathy with the ideas of the romantic novelist. (239)

Emma, recognizing and accepting her emotional needs, is finally not so different from Mildred Lathbury. Equipped with an entirely different personality and perspective, living in a time of radically expanded options for a woman, our modern heroine has in common with her elder sister the need for fulfillment in love.

The "nebulous, comfortable—even handsome—figure" that Emma wants in her future may very well be Tom, with whom she has been gradually developing a comfortable rela-tionship. Made dimly unhappy by Graham's presence in the village, he was unobtrusively and ineffectually interested in Emma from the beginning. As it did for Emma, the past comes into Tom's present, enabling him also to recover a vital aspect of himself. The agent of this beneficent fate is the feisty Daphne, who decides she has had it with duty and goes off to live in Birmingham with her bossy friend Heather and Bruce, her newly acquired dog. Daphne's decision to act according to her own needs and desires functions like a time machine that flings Tom back into a former identity: he is again an eligible widower, but one forced this time around to decide what he wants for himself. The direction of his thoughts is clear when he reads the obituary of a stranger, Fabian Charlesworth Driver, "Devoted husband of Constance and Jessie." Tom's curiosity about which wife this man will be buried with leads to a more personal consideration: "But supposing *he* were to marry again, as this man Driver must have done, what would be the position then?"

As insight seems to follow from failure for Emma, so it does for Tom. The crisis about Terry Skate's loss of faith, in which Tom can do nothing but admit defeat, turns into a crisis of his own, during which he wonders if "the whole business," the Christian faith, "wasn't an elaborate fiction." His momentary doubts are resolved by images. The first reveals the undeniable difference between the past and the present, the second discloses the potential for the renewal of the past in the present. As he chats with Miss Lee while she polishes the eagle lectern in the church, Tom remembers that it is not made of brass, as he has been thinking, but of wood. He realizes that he has failed to see what is actually before him because he was remembering "the church of his childhood." When he moves on to Miss Grundy, who is doing the altar flowers, working with the roses from the previous week, she gives him an even more important insight by remarking, "I think these [roses] will do another week, with a few more leaves. A few green leaves can make such a difference." Traditionally, the Church is the Rose of Sharon, and the importance of Miss Grundy's homely words is not lost on Tom. Most appropriately, he thinks she might be "the one person who could raise corn from the grains of wheat found in the wrappings of a mummy." She and Miss Lee have already worked the minor miracles of showing Tom that his church is not the Church of the past, but that, given the addition of a fresh and living faith, it need not be less beautiful, serviceable, and rewarding for that.

When Miss Lickerish dies, Tom feels that he comes "into his own," but in fact he has progressed steadily (and almost stealthily) since Daphne left. Miss Vereker's accidental location of the D.M.V. rid him of one major preoccupation with the past, and, by the gift of brandy to his organist, he made a little effort to improve his church. The need to fend for himself in the kitchen put him in touch, as a dinner guest, with some of his parishioners. And Miss Lickerish's death, an event with which only the rector can deal, reminds Tom that even in a world of doctors and social workers, only the clergyman deals with faith and human souls. To the extent that his quiet personality allows, he is past excessive diffidence, ready to see the need for his ministrations that has always been there. Earlier in the novel, Mrs. Furse spoke with "unexpected bitterness" about "all this history he's always going on about," and one of Martin's patients stunned the doctor into indignation by asking "if he believed in life after death."

Tom's readiness to let go of the historical past and his acceptance of the present is evident in his acceptance of Dr. Gellibrand and his talk to the history group—a talk in which the doctor resolutely ignores the "history of medical practices from the seventeenth century." Afterward, Tom checks discreetly whether Graham is permanently out of the picture and invites Emma to speak to the group, giving her a choice. She can talk about her recent observations on the village, perhaps relating them "to things that happened in the past . . . or even speculate on the future—what *might* happen in the years to come." Emma does not indicate which she will do, but in her last thoughts the future predominates:

> She remembered that her mother had said something about wanting to let the cottage to a former student, who was writing a novel and recovering from an unhappy love affair. But this was not going to happen, for Emma was going to stay in the village herself. *She* could write a novel and even, as she was beginning to realise, embark on a love affair which need not necessarily be an unhappy one. (249–50)

In Emma's fantastic idea that she might become a novelist are her rejection of the role of detached observer and her admission of the importance of the emotional life. Imagination enables her to see the possibility of change in herself and in how she relates to others. She chooses a new way of fitting into the community, which has already shown its acceptance of her by *expecting* her attendance at Miss Lickerish's funeral.

Beatrix's determination to be like "a kind of female villain" in a Victorian novel, foiling any idea Daphne might have of returning to her duty at the rectory, is completely unnecessary. Emma and Tom have made the most important decision anyone can make in Pym's world, deliberately choosing involvement over detachment, potential fulfillment over the unawareness of emotional need. In *A Few Green Leaves*, Pym acknowledges that the world has changed since the days when the young novelist wrote about Henry Hoccleve and Belinda and Harriet Bede. The foundations on which the social fabric rests are different, the behavior, the self-conceptions, and the options for the personal fulfillment of women and men are different. But amid all these changes, some things endure, and the most important are faith and love.

*   *   *

Though *The Sweet Dove Died* and *Quartet in Autumn* are very different, both are about the denial, because of pride and its corollary of self-sufficiency, of emotional need; both show that "romance" can inhibit the expression of unifying love. Meg is Pym's spokeswoman in the first novel, defining love by her attitude toward Colin and her remarks to Leonora, statements that apply to sexual or asexual love in all their varieties. She, Humphrey, and Liz demonstrate the ways people are taken out of themselves by the affection and concern for others or for animals. They experience aspects of the self that can never be known or experienced in isolation, and by doing this become full citizens of a world imperfect but still capable through love of satisfaction and fulfillment. The rejection of love for its imperfection is the rejection of life, and Leonora's choice to remain aloof diminishes her into an object as brittle and lifeless as the ones she dusts.

This novel is not unusual for the kind of attachment it details; it is Harriet and Mr. Donne again, though in a radically different key. What is special about it is the psychological portrait of Leonora. Although her life is a sterile existence, she does not see it as emptiness; instead, she sees it as a life uncluttered by signs of unbecoming needs, as proof of her superiority to others. Leonora, whose pride is shown to be self-admiration, cannot admire herself if she implicitly admits need by accepting the imperfect affection of an imperfect person. The need for love she discovers in herself she considers a flaw, and her reaction is to deny it. No cat, inconstant young man, or other "child substitute" will suggest to the world that Leonora Eyre needs something, anything other than herself. The proud woman needs nothing.

The denial of need in *Quartet in Autumn* is also the result of pride and ideas about self-sufficiency, but is complicated by Pym's emphasis on the general social pressures to conform to the isolating notions. In this novel, pride is the pretense that everything about oneself and one's life is fine— that one has no needs. In the lives of the quartet, the values of independence and privacy are related to pride and mean being blind to the others' needs as well as being mute about their own. The creed of this world where no one wants to know of another's troubles or betray his own is "don't get involved": it is not socially smart to acknowledge that someone else needs help or to suggest that one needs it, either. As the women's working days draw to a close, the members of the quartet, each isolated in his privacy and independence, do not realize how central their unacknowledged community has been to lives devoid of any other emotional focus. Letty wanted to be loved and never was. Marcia, on the other hand, may have hoped to be loved by Norman, but feels more acutely the lack of something to love since the death of Snowy. Her withdrawal into imbalance suggests that Marcia's need is greater than Letty's: it is important to be loved, but imperative to love.

Leonora's ideas about the kind of self-enhancing love she *can* accept are romantic. She wishes to acquire James, at first, as the perfect accoutrement for the mature attractive woman: it is proper, a tribute to herself, that she should have a young admirer. Unsought, loves comes to her, and it almost has to take the form of James—she could not love any man (like Humphrey) whose suitability would threaten to require genuine involvement or a commitment from her. Disarmed by James's youth and obvious "unsuitability" as a conventional romantic choice, she falls in love. Unfortunately, her obsession joins with her love to create some perverse romantic needs: he must be the perfect lover and theirs the perfect relationship. After all, if she is the perfect woman, fascinating and ageless, he should not want anyone else. Leonora must not only come first, she must be everything to James. Eventually, her suffering causes her to experience connection with others, people who are imperfect, fragile—and superfluous from the limited perspective of youthful beauty and romance. But she draws back from the unifying vision.

To stress that romantic love is one manifestation only of the need to establish emotional connection, Pym presents characters in their sixties in *Quartet in Autumn*. They are at an age when they no longer consider romantic love a possibility. Norman and Edwin laugh nervously at any suggestion that there might be something between them and the women, and their fear of giving even the appearance of romantic interest impedes their ordinary human responsiveness to the women. It is not the lack of a romantic object that destroys Marcia, but the lack of any form of emotional involvement. What there is besides romantic love that enables the extension of self is made clear by the novel: the little community, the Church, friendship, or even a pet. It takes pitifully little to satisfy the need for emotional connection or fulfillment, but needs not acknowledged or understood cannot be satisfied; Pym suggests that unexamined notions of self-sufficiency and pride can only be self-defeating for people who cannot live without each other.

In *A Few Green Leaves*, Tom and Emma do not deny their emotional needs out of pride or any great personal flaw; contemporary women and men do not necessarily define themselves according to their relationship to the opposite sex. They are more likely to define themselves according to their work. Emma has no awareness of emotional needs. What she does need, according to herself, is detachment for the sake of her work. Tom's perceived needs also center around work—he must figure out just what his job is and what it entails. Emma's unacknowledged need for love surfaces in her summons of the unappetizing Graham. Although the relationship gives her so little that it is not a good option for emotional fulfillment, it helps bring her to the recognition of her needs, and once she has understood what she wants for herself, she can stop being an observer. Tom's discovery of his needs is brought about by Daphne's departure. Forced for the first time to experience solitude and to decide how he wants to live, Tom is brought to the understanding that he wants love, and he too is rescued from a life of observation. Through Tom, Pym brings to the foreground the religious faith that has been in the background so often as an important aspect of her characters' lives. The renewal of Tom's emotional life, involved and intertwined with the renewal of his faith, points to the regenerative power of love.

*   *   *

Recently, I read a "human-interest" story in the newspaper about the wedding, in a nursing home, of a man and woman in their late seventies. The account included a quotation from Erich Fromm that was printed in the couple's wedding program: "Love is not primarily a relationship to a specific person; it is an attitude, an orientation of character which determines the relatedness of a person to the world as a whole." That is it exactly, the insight that animates and unifies Barbara Pym's novels. For that is the most remarkable aspect of Pym's achievement, the creation of a morally and artistically consistent little world with the power to expand our understanding of the larger one we inhabit. From the time we start reading about Belinda Bede until we end with Emma Howick and Tom Dagnall, we progress through time in the same world inhabited by people of a common background, sensibility, value system, and faith. As time moves along, some of the values shift here and there into different positions relative to each other and people's behavior changes accordingly, but it is still recognizably the same world in which we started, and it still elucidates our own.

Barbara Pym's finest novels are *The Sweet Dove Died* and *Quartet in Autumn*, and not only because they are "serious" novels, and, as such, suitable vehicles for the exposition of serious subjects. They are outstanding among the rest because, as the works which disclose and explore her vision most fully, they best convey the sense of urgency that led her to return again and again to the same themes. The impact of these novels is tremendous because Pym presents the issues and their primacy in a fashion more straightforward than comedy allows. They move us as Marcia and Leonora's fates unfold because their lives examine and illuminate our own. Especially in *Quartet,* it is impossible not to see the mirror held up before us, but Leonora's story also returns the shadow of our limitations and failures. Both novels present extreme situations, but Pym's triumph is that they reflect universal problems.

The moral vision that shapes these novels underlies and develops from the comedies. The most important thing that any of Pym's characters can do is choose whether or not to love, and they always make the choice whose expression can take many forms. From the beginning, Pym understood that her subject included but was not confined to romantic love and its successful issue. The comedies are very fine novels, and perhaps their greatest strength is the exclusion by satiric humor and irony of sentimentality in the treatment of the subject most capable of evoking latent mawkishness. Our laughter protects characters like Belinda Bede or Rupert Stonebird from an excessive pathos they do not deserve: the comedies celebrate their human resourcefulness and the dignity of all efforts, however zany or misguided, to satisfy their needs to love and be loved. Women and men acting on those needs merit our sympathy and admiration, funny though they frequently are.

A phrase from the hymn "New every morning is the love" is quoted by a couple of Pym's characters, but the whole couplet is important: "The trivial round, the common task / Will furnish all we ought to ask." The lines might describe Pym's chosen artistic materials: middle-class orderly people living lives undistinguished by awesome burdens or astonishing achievements. Hers are people actuated by garden-variety kindnesses, cruelties, fantasies, and needs, acting as often from the almost obsessive desire for social ease and smoothness as from the wish to do the "suitable" thing. Her achievement was to make these characters and their mundane actions reflect the most essential questions about the nature of life and love; her success, to demonstrate that such matters are not the province only of the great heroes and heroines of fiction or history but are the questions confronting ordinary people living ordinary lives everywhere, whose answers, implicitly or explicitly given, determine the quality and texture of life. By their very ordinariness, Pym's people represent humanity in the process of deciding just what kind of life it will live, what will be the nature of existence in an imperfect world that sometimes seems inimical to emotional fulfillment and happiness. Some of them turn away from the questions or, facing them, give the self-defeating, isolating answers; happily, most celebrate life and themselves in the decision to extend, through the various kinds of love, the vital bridge between the solitary self and the world.